Let Us Run The Race

Sheila Alewine
www.aroundthecornerministries.org

Around The Corner Ministries exists to take the gospel to every neighborhood in America. Our mission is to equip followers of Jesus to engage their neighborhoods and communities with the gospel of Jesus Christ.

© 2019 by Sheila Alewine

All rights reserved. No part of this publication may be reproduced in any form without the written permission of Around The Corner Ministries, P.O. Box 242, Etowah, NC 28739. www.aroundthecornerministries.org.

ISBN: 978-1-7330478-0-7

Scripture quotations taken from the New American Standard Bible® (NASB), Copyright © 1960, 1962, 1963, 1968, 1971, 1972, 1973, 1975, 1977, 1995 by The Lockman Foundation. Used by permission. www.Lockman.org.

*Inspired by Dave & Shelia and
their courageous team of World Racers.*

* * *

*Dedicated to all those
who run the race of life
with a passion for the gospel
and a love for Jesus.*

*Yet those who wait for the LORD will gain new strength;
they will mount up with wings like eagles,
they will run and not get tired,
they will walk and not become weary.
Isaiah 40:31*

A Word To The Reader

Therefore, since we have so great a cloud of witnesses surrounding us, let us also lay aside every encumbrance and the sin which so easily entangles us, and let us run with endurance the race that is set before us, fixing our eyes on Jesus, the author and perfecter of faith, who for the joy set before Him endured the cross, despising the shame, and has sat down at the right hand of the throne of God. For consider Him who has endured such hostility by sinners against Himself, so that you will not grow weary and lose heart.
Hebrews 12:1-3

"Let us run the race."

What encouraging words from the author of Hebrews, and what a beautiful picture that motivates and inspires us as we pursue a life dedicated to kingdom work. Each one of us has an individual path to run, and a purpose to accomplish while we are on earth, but we are all running toward the same finish line.

The word "race" is a metaphor. It describes the "persevering activity in the Christian course with a view to obtaining the reward; to strive hard; to exert oneself; to spend one's strength." The original Greek word is *trechō*, meaning "to incur extreme peril, which it requires the exertion of all one's effort to overcome."[1]

Even when we have trained well, are prepared mentally, physically and spiritually, and have our eyes firmly fixed on the goal, this race can be daunting. We will grow tired. We will get discouraged. We may feel at times as though we are "off course," stumbling through thorny obstacles and called upon to blaze a trail where no one has gone before. The writer of Hebrews knew this and gives us hope as we follow his instructions to keep our eyes on Jesus, the author and perfecter of our faith.

It is only in pursuing Christ Himself that we find the reward and can run the race with joy.

Over the next thirty days together, we will examine wisdom and insight from the apostle Paul's letter to the church at Philippi. Called the greatest missionary of all time, he made an unforgettable and enduring impact on the world and the culture that surrounded him. If we could sit down and chat with him, what would he tell us? What can we learn from a man who ran his race so well?

All of us desire to make our lives count for something greater than ourselves. The reality is, there is no greater call than the cause of Christ and the gospel of His kingdom. As Paul will teach us, let's pursue Him with passion, endurance and joy.

Let's run the race, for Jesus is worthy.

Day 1: Understand The Real Goal

But whatever things were gain to me, those things I have counted as loss for the sake of Christ. More than that, I count all things to be loss in view of the surpassing value of knowing Christ Jesus my Lord, for whom I have suffered the loss of all things, and count them but rubbish so that I may gain Christ, and may be found in Him, not having a righteousness of my own derived from the Law, but that which is through faith in Christ, the righteousness which comes from God on the basis of faith, that I may know Him and the power of His resurrection and the fellowship of His sufferings, being conformed to His death; in order that I may attain to the resurrection from the dead.
Philippians 3:7-11

What is the one thing that you really want out of life? If I asked you to describe a life that had meaning and purpose, what would you say?

Mainstream culture tells you that a successful life is achieved through beauty, money, pleasure, and power. Don't get me wrong; the world knows that generosity and service provide a sense of fulfillment. Doing good, fighting for social justice, defending the oppressed, feeding the hungry…everyone knows we should use our influence to help others. These things are good and right; the Bible tells us we should give to the poor, care for widows and orphans, and relieve physical suffering.

The difference for the Christ-follower is the "why" behind what we do.

Paul gives us the secret to having a life with purpose by comparing what he used to have with what he now has in Christ. He uses a very strong word translated as "rubbish" or "dung." In cultural context, it refers to the leftovers after a feast, which would be thrown to the dogs.[1]

What were the things that were previously **gain to him** that are now counted as **loss**? The answer is in his list of all his human accomplishments: his previous life as a Jewish rabbi, all of his education and training, all of the prestige, all of the status because of his family heritage, and even his impeccable record of blamelessly keeping the law (his good deeds). He's making a point. The real feast in life is knowing Christ. In comparison, everything else is rubbish, not worth keeping.

That's the goal of the race: knowing Christ. The goal is not accomplishing good deeds, although a person who knows Christ will do many good deeds. The goal is not fighting for social justice, although a person who knows Christ will be concerned about injustice. The goal is not leaving our mark on the world, although a person who knows Christ will influence many.

The goal is knowing Christ.

If knowing Christ is our end goal, then we must adjust our lives to run the race with that perspective. Paul tells us how.

Recognize the superior, surpassing value of Christ.

Knowing Christ is not something to achieve; He is a Person to know. And not just an ordinary person. He is the Son of God, the Savior, who gave His life so that we could enjoy a relationship with Him. He secured your eternal life, and then opened your eyes to understand your need of Him. Every temporary pleasure, every human achievement, pales in comparison to the value of knowing the Almighty Creator who desires to live in and through you.

Be prepared to lose everything.

When you recognize the greater value of something, you don't hesitate to exchange the less desirable in order to gain it. Paul says that he suffered the loss of all things. He's speaking from experience. In fact, he's speaking from prison! And yet, in light of losing his prestige, his reputation, his financial security, and even his life, he assures us that knowing Christ is far greater, and worth the sacrifice.

Jeremiah 9:23-24 – *Thus says the Lord, "Let not a wise man boast of his wisdom, and let not the mighty man boast of his might, let not a rich man boast of his riches; but let him who boasts, boast of this, that he understands and knows Me, that I am the Lord who exercises lovingkindness, justice and righteousness on earth; for I delight in these things," declares the Lord.*

Making It Personal

What is the difference in simply being acquainted with Christ and living your life with the purpose of knowing Him? How valuable is knowing Christ to you? What are you willing to give up?

Pray Today

Dear Jesus, Thank you for introducing Yourself to me! You pursued me, opened my eyes to understand the gospel, and called me to serve and follow You. What greater privilege in life is there than to know You? I ask You to teach me what it means to truly know You, as I run my race with perseverance and joy, fixing my eyes on You. Amen.

Day 2: To Know Him Is To Love Him

And this I pray, that your love may abound still more and more in real knowledge and all discernment. Philippians 1:9

That I may know Him and the power of His resurrection and the fellowship of His sufferings, being conformed to His death. Philippians 3:10

Paul presents an exciting proposition in his opening words to the Philippian believers. Our knowledge of God can grow, and as it grows, it affects how we love Him, and love others. To know Christ personally and intimately affects us from the inside out.

As believers, we have met Christ. The Spirit of God convicted us of our sin, and we repented, recognizing Jesus as the Son of God who paid our sin debt on the cross. We say now, that we *know* Christ. But knowledge is not stagnant, and the Christian life is not just a one-time acknowledgement of certain truths, after which we go on in life trying to do our best, to be a "good" Christian. Instead, following Christ is a life-long commitment to discovering who God is, how He works, and what He desires. It is a pursuit of real knowledge that is rooted in the word of God (what God has revealed about Himself) and experienced by obedience to the word of God, in relationship to Christ.

The word Paul uses for "knowledge" is *epignosis*, defined as "discernment or recognition." It expresses a sense of participation in the acquiring of knowledge. In other words, if we are going to know God fully, we must get out of the classroom and into the field. We must take the truths we know *about* Him and put them into practical use. If what we know about God doesn't affect our decisions, our thoughts, and our actions, then Christianity is just a theory. Real knowledge comes with application.

What kind of application does Paul tell us brings real knowledge? In Philippians 3:10 he gives three things to consider in our goal of knowing Christ.

We know Christ by experiencing the power of His resurrection.

Resurrection speaks of moving from death to life. It's the impossible made possible. Before salvation, we were dead in our sins, but Christ made us alive by grace through faith (Ephesians 2:1-6). This same power that raised Christ from the dead is at work in us, changing us into His image and empowering us for the work He calls us to do (Ephesians 1:19). This power, in the person of God's Holy Spirit, is the source of our sanctification. His indwelling Spirit gives us the desire to know God; He enlightens our finite minds to understand scripture, and then empowers us to obey it (Romans 8:11). We come to know Christ intimately as we learn to listen to, obey and walk according to the Spirit who has given us new life.

We know Christ by sharing in His sufferings.

Nothing increases our intimacy with God like suffering, because suffering fosters dependence. How did Christ suffer? He was rejected, belittled, and mocked. He lacked physical comfort, with no permanent home. He had to leave his Father's house and set aside His status. He was misunderstood and misquoted. He came to help and heal, to serve, and to save, but even His own brothers didn't believe in Him. His heart was grieved over the sins of His people. God promises that those who desire to run the race with godliness and integrity, pursuing Christ alone, will be persecuted (2 Timothy 3:12). We will come to know Christ more intimately in our moments of suffering than we ever will in our moments of comfort and ease.

We know Christ by being conformed to His death.

Jesus' earthly race did not end in death, and neither will ours. Physical death is simply something we must pass through. But we do die daily, as we deny ourselves, take up our cross, and follow Him (Matthew 16:24). The old self, our sinful nature, was crucified with Christ, and we walk in newness of life (Romans 6:4-6). We know God as we allow Him to transform us into His likeness. We are no longer conformed to the world, but present ourselves as a *living and holy sacrifice*, and so we are conformed to His death (Romans 12:1-2).

Can you see that following Christ is a life-long pursuit, a race to run focused only on knowing Him, knowing His Word, and living it out in practical, everyday obedience? We aren't pursuing knowledge; we are pursuing Him. The amazing thing is, He never stops pursuing your heart. The Father loves you and wants you to know Him. Jesus came to reveal Him and make it possible, and the Spirit dwells in you, enlightening your mind to understand the Word, guiding, directing, convicting and shaping you into His image.

1 John 5:20 – *And we know that the Son of God has come, and has given us understanding so that we may know Him who is true; and we are in Him who is true, in His Son Jesus Christ. This is the true God and eternal life.*

Making It Personal

How well do you know Him? What will you do today to know Him more?

Pray Today

Dear Jesus, We want to know you! Teach us to spend our days in pursuit of You. Let our lives be an example of Your resurrection power as it conforms us to You. May we be willing to die to ourselves so that we may know You more. Amen.

Day 3: Experience Resurrection Power

That I may know Him and the power of His resurrection.
Philippians 3:10a

But if the Spirit of Him who raised Jesus from the dead dwells in you, He who raised Christ Jesus from the dead will also give life to your mortal bodies through His Spirit who dwells in you.
Romans 8:11

The resurrection of Jesus sets the Christian faith apart from all other religions. Paul told the Corinthian believers that if Jesus was not resurrected, then our faith is worthless. (1 Corinthians 15:17-19). He knew that the fact of the resurrection was foundational to everything we believe and experience about God.

Consider how powerful this truth is. What is the one thing that humanity cannot overcome? It doesn't matter how much money you have, how smart you are, how healthy you eat, how hard you exercise, how many vitamins you take. The reality of life is that our bodies will die. In fact, before you were born, God already wrote down the day your physical body will stop functioning and you will leave this physical realm to step into eternity (Psalm 139:16). Your soul, however, will live forever because it is immortal. It will either go to live in heaven with God, awaiting the resurrection of your physical body, or it will spend eternity in darkness, separated from God forever.

The same power that gives us hope for the resurrection of our bodies also gives us spiritual life here on earth. After God created man's physical body, He breathed into him the breath of life, the spirit and soul. Your soul is that unseen, inner part of you that makes you unique and distinct from every other person. It is your personality, your will, and your emotions. The spirit of man is the part of us that communicates with God's Spirit (Romans 8:16) and it is that part of us which died when sin came into the world, and it is what is brought to life by the Spirit of God Himself at salvation (1 John 4:13). Unsaved men have a body and a soul, but their spirit is not alive to God.

Ephesians 2 tells us before Christ, we were dead in our trespasses and sins. What was dead? Not our physical bodies; we were upright, walking, breathing and talking. Not our souls; we had thought, emotion, and will. It was our spirit that was dead. God is a Spirit, and before our spirits received life from His Spirit, we had no way to communicate with Him, or raise ourselves up. We needed resurrection power, the same power that raised Christ from the dead. We needed the life that only the Spirit of God can provide.

The power of the resurrection that Paul so longed to experience and know is the life-giving, indwelling Holy Spirit who enables us to live for God here on earth and who will carry us into the presence of God when we die.

How is this power realized in our day-to-day lives?

Resurrection power…
…allows us to resist temptation and overcome sin (1 Corinthians 10:13).
…gives us courage in the face of impossible circumstances (2 Timothy 1:7).
…enables us to speak the gospel boldly (Ephesians 6:20).
…makes unity possible with our brothers and sisters in Christ (Ephesians 4:3).

This resurrection power is so powerful it enables us to know God intimately, to be one with Him just as He and the Father are one (John 17:21-23). No wonder Paul was able to overcome every obstacle the enemy placed in his path. Nothing on earth is greater than resurrection power!

Ephesians 1:18-21 – *I pray that the eyes of your heart may be enlightened, so that you will know what is the hope of His calling, what are the riches of the glory of His inheritance in the saints, and what is the surpassing greatness of His power toward us who believe. These are in accordance with the working of the strength of His might which He brought about in Christ, when He raised Him from the dead and seated Him at His right hand in the heavenly places, far above all rule an authority and power and dominion, and every name that is named, not only in this age, but also in the one to come.*

Making It Personal

What difference has the power of the resurrection made in your life? What are you struggling with today that needs the resurrection power of the Spirit of God? Who has God has put in your life that needs to know about resurrection power? Will you tell them?

Pray Today

Dear Jesus, We need resurrection power in our lives! How grateful we are for the assurance that You are alive, that the grave could not hold you. This assurance comes as Your Spirit, alive and dwelling in us, bears testimony that we are Your children and that You have called us as Your own. Your Spirit spoke to us, and we responded. Teach us to live in the power of the resurrection, confident that You are able to handle everything that comes our way by Your sovereign hand. May we spend our lives pursuing You, and truly know the power of Your resurrection. Amen.

Day 4: Be Willing To Suffer With Christ

That I may know Him and the power of His resurrection and the fellowship of His sufferings, being conformed to His death; in order that I may attain to the resurrection from the dead.
Philippians 3:10-11

How would you respond if someone offered you the chance to become an authority on the subject of suffering? I'm sure you would probably decline this opportunity. But what if I told you that is the only way you'll truly know God intimately and personally? Would you embrace it? Or run from it?

When Paul met Jesus on the road to Damascus, he started a life-long journey of suffering. After his "face to face" experience with Jesus, he was led by the hand into the city, to sit and wait in the darkness, blinded by the light of heaven. Ananias was told by God to go and lay hands on him, and that God was going to "show him how much he must suffer for My name's sake."

How did Paul suffer? He was beaten, imprisoned, falsely accused, shipwrecked, and threatened. He was run out of town on multiple occasions. His own people rejected him and despised his teaching. He experienced hunger and cold and at times despaired of life. He was plagued by spiritual attacks. Yet, he never turned away from God, never gave up sharing the gospel, and never regretted that God had called him and saved him.

In fact, Paul embraced his suffering, and even rejoiced in it. That sounds like he had lost his mind, doesn't it? What possible joy could there be in suffering for the cause of Christ? What purpose could God have in allowing it?

Paul knew the secret. Suffering for the cause of Christ identifies us with our Savior. We share in His suffering. We are made aware of the cost of our redemption in a very real, tangible way. We come to know Him more intimately, and we genuinely experience Him as He comforts us, gives us peace, and in our most difficult times, sustains us by His grace and the presence of His Spirit.

Paul knew that suffering opened the door of opportunity for God to be glorified, and for him to experience the power of God in very personal ways. His faith in God, and his knowledge of God grew in direct proportion to his suffering.

Suffering causes us to depend on God. The truth is, we have little, if any, control over our lives. We have free will to make choices, but ultimately, God has sovereign power over all. When things are going smoothly, we don't seem to need God quite as much. But when we receive a troubling diagnosis, or someone we care about leaves us, or when everything we try seems to fail, or when we can't pay our bills, or when we are rejected or mocked for our faith, suddenly the nearness of God is something we crave. Like Paul, we realize that suffering isn't to be avoided, but embraced as God's way of revealing Himself to us and bringing us into intimate fellowship with Him.

1 Peter 4:12-13 - *Beloved, do not be surprised at the fiery ordeal among you, which comes upon you for your testing, as though some strange thing were happening to you; but to the degree that you share the sufferings of Christ, keep on rejoicing, so that also at the revelation of His glory you may rejoice with exultation.*

Making It Personal

What has suffering taught you in the past about God? Are you suffering today? How is what you are experiencing today bringing you closer to the Savior?

Pray Today

Dear Jesus, How we want to know You! But the path to intimacy with You is not an easy one. You warned us that this world would be filled with tribulation and suffering, but You also promised us that You would never leave us in those trials. Teach us to embrace the hard days as opportunities for us to lean into You, trust You, and get to know You. We ask that You use all of our suffering to bring glory to Yourself and conform us to You. Help us to have grateful hearts in the hard places and rejoice that we are counted worthy to suffer for Your name. Amen.

Day 5: Be Conformed To His Death

*...that I may know Him and the power of His resurrection
and the fellowship of His sufferings, being conformed to His death;
in order that I may attain to the resurrection from the dead.*
Philippians 3:10-11

Paul told us that his goal in life, what made him successful in his calling, was to focus all his energy, time, talent, and resources on knowing Christ. He also told us two specific ways we come to know Christ. First, by the power of the resurrection, where we are given spiritual life at salvation, and filled with the power of the Holy Spirit for this new life. Second, by suffering with Christ, where we surrender our lives to God's plans, unwilling to hold back anything and refusing to cling to the comforts of this world, for the sake of Christ.

As we commit ourselves to knowing Christ, something happens **to** us. We find ourselves **being conformed** to His death. "Being conformed" is translated from the Greek word *symmorphizō* and means "to receive the same form as," to "render like." The present passive tense of the word indicates this is an on-going process, and it is something that happens to us, as a result of something else.[1]

Paul is speaking about the death of our old self, our flesh. Our spirit is alive to Christ, but we still live in an unredeemed human body. Our soul (our emotions, will, desires) is torn between following the Spirit of God who lives in us, and the fallen, human flesh. Paul even calls it a war (Romans 7:23). We've all experienced it. Even though we love God and have given ourselves to Him, we fight a daily battle to put to death our flesh and be transformed into the image of Christ.

To understand the power of what Paul is teaching us we need to remember what Christ's death accomplished. His death on the cross defeated the power of sin. Sin has consequences; it requires a blood payment (Romans 3:23-25). When Christ died, payment was made. When the blood is applied to our account at salvation, sin no longer has any power over us. But even though we are free from the penalty and power of sin, we still live in its presence, and are influenced by it. Being conformed to Christ's death means that we are daily putting to death the deeds of the body (Romans 8:13). In essence, as we grow in our knowledge of Christ and are transformed into His likeness, we allow Him to "finish the job" in us personally. This is why Paul says we share in the suffering of Christ. He suffered to end sin's power, and now our earthly suffering works to end sin's lingering effects in our flesh. Thus, we are **conformed to His death.**

Elsewhere in scripture (Colossians 3), Paul gives the illustration of putting off the old life (*suffering*) and putting on the new life (*resurrection*). The physical act of Christ's death on the cross, His burial, and His resurrection is played out again and again in every believer as we die to our old lives and are raised to live as transformed people. This new life is the abundant life, the life of truly knowing Christ.

The good news is that this is an on-going process, carried out in us **as we fulfill the calling and mission** God has given us. If we were running a physical marathon, we would have to train for months prior to the race. We would need to arrive at a certain level of physical fitness before we could even attempt to compete. But the Christian life *is the race*. The training, the transformation, happens during the race. The goal is knowing Christ, and our particular mission or task is simply the path that God has planned for us to know Him more today, until we know Him fully in eternity.

Philippians 3:20-21 – *For our citizenship is in heaven, from which also we eagerly wait for a Savior, the Lord Jesus Christ; who will transform the body of our humble state into conformity with the body of His glory, by the exertion of the power that He has even to subject all things to Himself.*

Making It Personal

As a Christ-follower, in what areas of your life are you aware of God's transforming work? How is He changing you, transforming you into His image? Are there areas where you are resistant to being conformed to His death? What will you do about them today?

Pray Today

Dear Jesus, How grateful we are that You finished the work of defeating the power of sin. You took away its hold on us, and we no longer stand accused or guilty. Help us to understand what it means to be conformed to Your death, as we surrender ourselves to You daily, putting to death what our old flesh desires. As we grow in our knowledge of You, we trust that we will run our race well, accomplishing all that You have purposed for us. Amen.

Day 6: You're Not Alone

I thank my God in all my remembrance of you,
always offering prayer with joy in my every prayer for you all,
in view of your participation in the gospel from the first day until now.
Philippians 1:3-5

How does it make you feel when someone tells you they are praying for you? How you respond will be directly related to what you believe about prayer. If we believe that God truly hears the prayers of His children, and that He is moved by them, then we are encouraged, humbled and excited to know that someone is talking to God about us. But if we think prayer is just some spiritual exercise to make ourselves feel better, then knowing someone is praying for you has little encouragement or effect.

Paul knew that in his absence, the most powerful thing he could do for his believing friends was to pray for them. It's the first thing he tells them in this letter, after greeting them. He wanted them to know that they were not alone in their struggles to hold fast to their faith. They were facing persecution, struggling with unity and sharp disagreements within the church, and plagued by false teachers. He knew exactly what they were feeling and experiencing, yet he found great joy every time he prayed for them. Why? Because they were partners with him in the gospel. He knew the gospel that had saved them was able to carry them through any hardship, and that God would remain faithful to them.

Listen to these words: *It is only right for me to feel this way about you all, because I have you in my heart, since both in my imprisonment and in the defense and confirmation of the gospel, you all are partakers of grace with me* (Philippians 1:7).

You, too, are on a spiritual journey. God has called you for the "defense and confirmation of the gospel" whether you are in a foreign land or at home in your own city. Whether you are there for two weeks, a month, or the rest of your life, you are a partaker of grace, on the same mission as Paul. And according to Hebrews 12:1, we could even say that Paul is one of the faithful witnesses in heaven cheering you on.

Who else is praying for you?

You might have the support of family members and a church body who are regularly asking God to meet your needs and sustain you on your journey. Maybe it's just one or two good friends that you can count on, that you can text or email or call and know that they will be faithful to lift you up to the Father. But even if you can't think of a single person, I want to encourage you:

Jesus is praying for you!

According to scripture, Jesus is at the right hand of the Father, interceding for you (Hebrews 7:25, Romans 8:34). He is your advocate, talking to the Father on your behalf (1 John 2:1). And if you wonder what He might be praying for you, consider what He prayed in John 17:

He prayed for God to protect you.
He prayed for God to sanctify you.
He prayed for God to allow you to experience oneness and unity with Himself and the Father.
He prayed for your joy to be made full.

Sometimes we *feel* alone, but know this, my friend, you are not alone. The Spirit of God who indwells you is interceding for you and Jesus Himself is interceding for you. The Father knows, and sees, and hears, and you are not alone.

Romans 8:26 – *In the same way the Spirit also helps our weakness; for we do not know how to pray as we should, but the Spirit Himself intercedes for us with groanings too deep for words.*

Making It Personal

In what areas do you need prayer? If you have a prayer team, contact them and be specific in asking for prayer. Then, thank Jesus that He is already praying for you.

Pray Today

Dear Jesus, How reassuring and comforting to know that You are praying for us. We close our eyes and imagine the Father's throne room. If we could see past the glory and beauty, we would find You there, in communion with the Father and the Spirit, never missing a detail. May we find oneness with You. May You sanctify us, and fill us with Your joy, knowing that the Father is protecting us as we serve You. May the knowledge that You are interceding for us empower us as bold witnesses for the gospel today. Amen.

Day 7: It's Not You; It's Him

For I am confident of this very thing, that He who began a good work in you will perfect it until the day of Christ Jesus.
Philippians 1:6

...for it is God who is at work in you, both to will and to work for His good pleasure.
Philippians 2:13

How confident are you that you will be successful in the kingdom work to which you have been called? If you're trusting in your own abilities and skill, you have good reason to doubt the success of the mission. But if you're confidence is well-placed, in the God who calls and equips you, then you can wake up every morning fully confident that the day will be a success.

Who's doing the work, anyway?

We began this journey establishing why we run the race. We're seeking the Master, not the mission. We serve the King, not the kingdom. Our focus is centered on learning to know God, listening to His Spirit speak, and obeying when He prompts us. We are spending time in His word, learning how to live this new life. God is at work in us, perfecting what He started on the day He saved us. And in the process, He uses us to expand the kingdom and spread the gospel.

Paul had no doubt that what God had begun, He was able to complete. He had given up all confidence in his own ability to accomplish great things for God and surrendered to the knowledge that God was the One doing the work. It was His mission, His assignment. God had initiated the relationship and issued the call; Paul was simply a willing vessel to be used.

The word Paul used for "perfect" doesn't mean that everything you do for God will be flawless. God is perfect; we're not. We make mistakes. We get ahead of ourselves. We think much of ourselves instead of others. Paul is not expressing confidence in the believers' ability to perform well for God, but that God is working out His divine purposes through imperfect people. To "perfect" is to complete or to finish.[1] God doesn't abandon us when we don't measure up. He keeps on working in us and through us until He has accomplished what He intended.

Paul says it is God who works in us, both to **will** and to **work** for His good pleasure. In other words, God gives us the desire and the ability. It is not human to desire to be Christ-like. It is not in our flesh to love the gospel and want to share it with the world. And it is not in our ability that spiritual transformation will take place, either in us or in the people we serve. God gives us the motivation and desire, and then enables us by His Spirit to do the work.

It's not you; it's Him.

What does this do for our confidence level? Like Paul, it should sustain us through times of doubt, trials, and suffering. When we feel less than adequate for the task, we lean into Him, and draw our strength from His word and the presence of His Spirit. When we feel like we failed, we trust there is a lesson that will pay greater dividends in the future. We learn, day by day, moment by moment, that indeed, we are not capable of this great mission, but He is. And He intends to work through us, and in us, until the work is done, and He glorified.

Hebrews 13:20-21 – *Now the God of peace, who brought up from the dead the great Shepherd of the sheep through the blood of the eternal covenant, even Jesus our Lord, equip you in every good thing to do His will, working in us that which is pleasing in His sight, through Jesus Christ, to whom be the glory forever and ever. Amen.*

Making It Personal

Are there any areas of your life where you are a bit too confident in yourself? Are there places where you feel defeated? Surrender your feelings of pride or inadequacy to God. Let Him be the author of your desires and abilities to work for Him.

Pray Today

Dear Jesus, We all want to measure up. We all want to feel needed, and important, and capable. We confess our tendency to depend on ourselves to accomplish things that can only be done by Your Spirit and Your power. Show us the places in our hearts that are filled with self-confidence and replace them with confidence in You alone. Only then will we be able to run with joy, knowing that You will perfect what You began in us. Amen.

Day 8: Holiness Matters

And this I pray, that your love may abound still more and more in real knowledge and discernment, so that you may approve the things that are excellent, in order to be sincere and blameless until the day of Christ; having been filled with the fruit of righteousness which comes through Jesus Christ, to the glory and praise of God.
Philippians 1:9-11

Paul knew the power of sin's influence. His letters are filled with warnings about overcoming the temptations of the world. Just in this letter to the Philippians, he speaks of living in a "manner worthy of the gospel" (1:27), proving ourselves to be blameless and innocent (2:15), living up to the standard (3:16), and having our minds dwell on what is true and honorable (4:8).

He also knew the power of personal influence. What we see in one another can either inspire us to holiness or entice us to sin. Paul was very conscious of conducting himself in a way that he could encourage others to emulate, and this is what he is telling us in these verses.

As our love for God grows, it abounds in real knowledge and discernment. Knowledge is gained by information; for example, what we learn by reading His Word and the clear conviction of the Spirit. Discernment is perception; we learn by observation. We see something and gain understanding.

What purpose does this knowledge and discernment serve? Paul tells us **so that** we may approve (test, examine or prove) what is excellent. The word translated as "excellent" means "to carry through, to make a difference, to distinguish, to excel, to be of more value." As believers, we must decide what is the greater value, **in order** to be sincere (pure, proven genuine) and blameless. Blameless here does not mean you are perfect. The word means "without offense, not causing someone to stumble." The picture is of a smooth road without stones.

Let's put it plainly. I love God, so I pursue knowledge of Him and what pleases Him. As I pursue Him, my love for my brother or sister in Christ grows. I see what is good and right in His Word. I observe what is going on in your life, and I make choices that provide the greater influence for your spiritual growth as well as mine. I determine to live in a way that you can follow my example to Christ. It helps "carry you through" to spiritual maturity. I resolve to give no opportunity for you to stumble in your walk with Christ.

I live intentionally, filled with Christ's righteousness, avoiding the influence of sin and recognizing the influence I have on others around me. Holiness matters because Christ died to make us holy.

Whether we are on mission with others in a foreign country, or simply doing life in our own city, we have influence on other believers and a world that needs to see a clear picture of Jesus. Paul calls us to examine our lives and prove our genuine faith. We set aside any idea of personal freedom that may cause another to stumble into sin and conduct ourselves in righteous living.

2 Corinthians 1:12 - *For our proud confidence is this: the testimony of our conscience, that in holiness and godly sincerity, not in fleshly wisdom but in the grace of God, we have conducted ourselves in the world, and especially toward you.*

Making It Personal

Is there anything in your life that could cause someone to stumble? Are you conscious that your personal choices have influence? Ask God to reveal anything in your life that isn't "excellent."

Pray Today

Dear Jesus, We live in a world with many influences. We need Your wisdom to be discerning. As we pursue knowing You, and loving You, may our hearts be sensitive to what is sinful, and compassionate toward our weaker brothers and sisters. Make us examples of Your righteousness, as we follow closely after You.

Day 9: Use Your Platform

Now I want you to know, brethren, that my circumstances have turned out for the greater progress of the gospel, so that my imprisonment in the cause of Christ has become well known throughout the whole praetorian guard and to everyone else, and that most of the brethren, trusting in the Lord because of my imprisonment, have far more courage to speak the word of God without fear.
Philippians 1:12-14

We've already talked a lot about suffering and its place in our lives. God uses suffering to not only shape us personally into the image of Christ, but how we respond to challenging circumstances can also have a great impact on others, especially those to whom we are preaching the gospel, both in our words and our deeds.

For most of his life, Paul's platform was suffering. He leveraged it for the gospel. A quick read through 2 Corinthians 11 and 12 reveals that carrying the gospel cost him dearly physically, emotionally and mentally. In contrast, his spiritual life overflowed with joy, because he knew without a doubt, he was following God's plan for his life. He was called to preach the gospel to the Gentiles, and so he capitalized on every opportunity, every platform God gave him, even in his suffering.

He was able to say with confidence, "my circumstances have turned out for the greater progress of the gospel."

Every Christ-follower has a platform. Listen to Paul's words in Acts 17:24-27:

The God who made the world and all things in it, since He is Lord of heaven and earth, does not dwell in temples made with hands; nor is He served by human hands, as though He needed anything, since He Himself gives to all people life and breath and all things; and He made from one man every nation of mankind to live on all the face of the earth, having determined their appointed times and the boundaries of their habitation, that they would seek God, if perhaps they might grope for Him and find Him, though He is not far from each one of us.

Did you catch that? God determined **when** you would live, **where** you would live, and **why** you would live. Your present circumstances, whether you are comfortably sitting at home or suffering in prison for your faith, or laboring in a foreign land for the gospel, are divinely orchestrated by God Himself. You are where you are so that you will seek God, and so that you will point others who are seeking Him to Jesus.

Don't waste your God-given platform by focusing only on the circumstances.

Instead, trust that God knows what He's doing, and ask Him to give you insight on how the very things that challenge you can become a platform for the gospel. Just like Joseph in the Old Testament, God allows our circumstances for our good, and His glory (Romans 8:28-30).

You may be thinking, "But you don't know my situation." And that's true, I don't. But God does. He not only knows where you are today, but how you got there. He's never lost sight of you. And no matter how bad your circumstances may seem in the moment, He has good plans for you, plans that will magnify the life-changing power of the gospel in your own anxious heart, as well as proclaim the gospel through you to a world that gropes for Him in the dark.

Luke 21:13 – *It will lead to an opportunity for your testimony.*

Making It Personal

What challenging circumstances are in your life today that God wants to use as a platform for the gospel? How will you see things differently?

Pray Today

Dear Jesus, Your life here on earth is a testimony to us that challenging circumstances are often the very thing that lead to the greatest victory. You used Your platform to not only preach about the kingdom of heaven, but surrendered Your life to obtain salvation for us. Because of Your finished work, we can trust our heavenly Father to use all things for His glory and our good. Teach us to look at our circumstances through the eyes of the gospel, and may we use every day as a platform for talking about You. Amen.

Day 10: You've Got Nothing To Lose

According to my earnest expectation and hope, that I will not be put to shame in anything, but that with all boldness, Christ will even now, as always, be exalted in my body, whether by life or by death. For to me, to live is Christ, and to die is gain.
Philippians 1:20-21

Paul lived with a sense of abandon. He had experienced success in the world's eyes, along with power and prestige, but when he encountered Jesus, he did not hesitate to exchange all of it for his new life in Christ. As he surrendered to preach the gospel, he gained a new purpose, a new identity, and a new future: eternal life with God in heaven.

Paul had nothing left to lose.

In his letter to the Galatians, Paul says, I have been crucified with Christ; and it is no longer I who live, but Christ lives in me; and the life which I now live in the flesh I live by faith in the Son of God, who loved me and gave Himself up for me (Galatians 2:20). In a very real way, his old life was dead, and he now sought to act and move only as the Spirit of God acted and moved through him. His life no longer belonged to him and every decision made was based on whether it would either magnify Christ or bring Him shame. In fact, he called himself a "bond-servant" – a word that describes someone who loves his master so much that he chooses to stay and serve Him for life, rather than go free.

Because his life belonged to Christ, he walked by faith, trusting that God would protect him, sustain him, and direct his steps in such a way that the gospel would be proclaimed, and Jesus would be magnified. If his life were to end, he trusted that God had concluded the purpose for his life; after all, it was God's life, not his.

When we know that we have nothing to lose we can live without fear. We can lay down at night and sleep, resting in the assurance that God has everything under control. We can give up grasping for things we think we need and trust the Father to provide. We can obey confidently and boldly, like Paul, trusting that Christ will be exalted either by our lives, or by our deaths.

How do we live with a sense of abandon like Paul?

Make much of Christ: *Christ will even now, as always, be exalted in my body.*

John the Baptist said it this way: *He must increase, but I must decrease* (John 3:30). Paul never wavered on the priority of making Jesus known. He knew that as long as Christ was magnified, he had nothing to fear. If he was killed, he would gain heaven. In fact, the harder thing was to remain and keep teaching and preaching, but he knew this would bring glory to God (Philippians 1:22-26). His desire was to enter heaven as a faithful servant, having used up every ounce of energy and life to point people to Jesus (2 Timothy 4:6-8).

Think much of Heaven: *To live is Christ, and to die is gain.*

The more we dwell on what is truly "gain" the less we fear our death, and the easier it is to let go of things and live with abandon. We realize that what the world thinks is the worst thing that could happen is for the believer, the best thing. The hope of stepping out of this world of sin and suffering into the eternal presence of our Savior fills us with excitement and anticipation, and even the good things in this life hold little attraction in comparison.

Work much for the kingdom: *But if I am to live on in the flesh, this will mean fruitful labor for me.*

We can work hard for the kingdom, knowing our inheritance is waiting, and this life is only temporary. For Paul, his work was preaching the gospel and equipping the believers. Each of us has gifts, talents, and God-given desires that are to be used to grow the body of Christ (Ephesians 4:16). We are all working in the same harvest but in different fields, at different times. Jesus said we are to *seek first His kingdom and His righteousness, and all these things will be added to you, because your heavenly Father knows that you need all these things.* (Paraphrased, see Matthew 6:25-34).

Run the race with abandon. Don't worry where the next bend in the road might take you. There will be challenges. You will face distractions. But that's not your problem. Just make much of Jesus, think much of heaven, and work much for the kingdom. You've got nothing to lose.

Mark 8:35 - *For whoever wishes to save his life will lose it, but whoever loses his life for My sake and the gospel's will save it.*

Making It Personal

Do you live with abandon, or are there things holding you back from fully surrendering to God's purpose for your life? What are you afraid of? Tell God your fears and ask Him to fill you with joy and confidence as you learn to walk by faith.

Pray Today

Dear Jesus, It is easy to find ourselves holding tightly to this world and all it offers. Teach us to count all things as loss, so that we have nothing to lose by following You with abandon, just as Paul did. You have promised us everything. Help us to magnify You in life, holding nothing back. Amen.

Day 11: Pursue A Gospel-Centered Unity

*Only conduct yourselves in a manner worthy of the gospel of Christ,
so that whether I come and see you or remain absent,
I will hear of you that you are standing firm in one spirit,
with one mind striving together for the faith of the gospel.*
Philippians 1:27

*Therefore if there is any encouragement in Christ,
if there is any consolation of love,
if there is any fellowship of the Spirit,
if any affection and compassion,
make my joy complete by being of the same mind,
maintaining the same love, united in spirit, intent on one purpose.*
Philippians 2:1-2

The Bible talks a lot about unity between brothers and sisters in Christ, and for good reason. Jesus said that this would be an undeniable testimony to the power of the gospel, and the presence of the Spirit that unites us. As He prayed for us in the Garden of Gethsemane, just before going to the cross, He asked His Father for to give the disciples (and all who would believe) the same kind of unity that Jesus Himself enjoyed with His Father! And He was crystal clear about its importance.

...that they may all be one; even as You, Father, are in Me and I in You, that they also may be in Us, **so that the world may believe that You sent Me.** The glory which You have given Me I have given to them, that they may be one, just as We are one; I in them and You in Me, that they may be perfected in unity, **so that the world may know that You sent Me, and loved them**, even as You have loved Me. (John 17:21-23)

The apostle John spoke strongly about unity in the body, telling us that if we hate our brother, we do not belong to Christ (1 John 2:9-11; 3:14-16). In other letters, Paul tells us to "be like-minded, live in peace" (2 Corinthians 13:11); we are instructed to "all agree, and that there be no divisions among us" but we are to be "made complete in the same mind and in the same judgment" (1 Corinthians 1:10. We are to be "diligent to preserve the unity of the Spirit in the bond of peace" (Ephesians 4:3) and to "put on love, which is the perfect bond of unity" (Colossians 3:14).

Unity matters because it testifies that Jesus is indeed alive, and He lives in us.

What unifies us? Biblical unity is not just a warm and fuzzy feeling. The world's version of unity is to look at one another and agree that anything and everything is good and acceptable, and that we should all unify around one another. But biblical unity is centered on Jesus. As Christ-followers seek to obey and serve Christ alone, we are drawn together **towards Christ.** We then become one body, one family, all moving in the same direction, led by the same Spirit of God who indwells us, committed to the same truth of God's Word, worshipping the same God and Father of us all.

Our love for Jesus, and our commitment to the gospel overrides the differences in our personalities and preferences. We surrender our need for independence and recognition, so that Christ is recognized. When the world sees people, who may have strong differences of opinion, but are willing to work in unity for the glory of God, then the gospel is clearly illustrated.

We strive together with the same mind, because we have the mind of Christ (1 Corinthians 2:16). We stand firm in one spirit, because we have the Holy Spirit (Romans 8:9-17). And we love one another as brothers and sisters, because we are children of the same Father who bestowed on us His great love (1 John 3:1).

Do you see how Christ's prayer in the Garden has been answered? We are truly made one, just as He asked. And so, the world will believe.

Psalm 133:1 - *Behold, how good and how pleasant it is For brothers to dwell together in unity!*

Making It Personal

Is there a lack of unity between you and any of your brothers or sisters in Christ? What can you do today to repair the relationship? How can the gospel fix the division between you?

Pray Today

Dear Jesus, It seems impossible that we could experience unity with our brothers and sisters the same way that You are one with the Father and the Spirit. Yet, this is what You prayed for us, so by faith, we believe it is truly possible. Help us to set aside any differences that are not central to the truth of the gospel and learn to live in unity. We want the world to know that You are the living Savior by the testimony of how we love each other. Thank You for Your Spirit who indwells us and knits our hearts together in You. Amen.

Day 12: Imitate Christ

> *Do nothing from selfishness or empty conceit,*
> *but with humility of mind regard one another as more important than yourselves;*
> *do not merely look out for your own personal interests,*
> *but also for the interests of others.*
> *Have this attitude in yourselves which was also in Christ Jesus, who,*
> *although He existed in the form of God, did not regard equality with God a thing to*
> *be grasped, but emptied Himself, taking the form of a bond-servant,*
> *and being made in the likeness of men. Being found in appearance as a man, He*
> *humbled Himself by becoming obedient to the point of death,*
> *even death on a cross.*
> Philippians 2:3-8

Yesterday we talked about the concept of unity that God desires His children to exhibit. Today, Paul teaches us how it can be worked out practically, and he uses the greatest example of all to show us how it can be done.

It's one thing to say we want unity; it's another thing to experience it, because the experience requires us to examine how we treat one another. Unity doesn't happen naturally, even in the body of Christ, because we are made of flesh, and prone to sin. Simply put, we want what we want! While the Spirit of God living in us empowers us and directs us towards unity, it must be put into practice in our words, our actions, our thoughts, and our attitudes about others.

Paul knew human nature, and so he doesn't hesitate to address the core of our issues: selfishness, conceit, pride, self-interest, and a desire for recognition. The Greek word translated "selfishness" means "a desire to put oneself forward." Empty conceit is a compound word that literally means "vain or empty glory." Human nature tends to focus on self; we're also likely to have an inflated view of ourselves. It's just how our fallen nature works.

In contrast, Jesus exhibited selflessness at every level. He laid aside all His glory to become human, so that we could understand who God is. He put our well-being ahead of His own, even humbling Himself to be suffer a painful death on the cross. He set aside all the privileges of being the Son of God, so that we could have the privilege of becoming children of God.

Paul urges us to imitate Christ, because only in imitating Him can we dwell in unity with one another. We are not to just look out for our own interests, but to look across the table at others and ask ourselves, what is best for *them*? Are we becoming a bondservant like Christ, or are we seeking our own comforts, fulfilling our own needs, and pursuing our own advancement?

It's not a coincidence that just after Paul taught the Roman believers to present their bodies a living sacrifice and allow God to transform their minds, that he talks about unity, specifically, that we are not to think more highly of ourselves, but to have sound judgment. In other words, only a mind transformed by Christ can see others with the compassion and care of Christ and think less of self. (Romans 12:1-3)

The good news is, we *can* live in peace with one another. When strife or discord or hurt feelings start to distract us, we simply go back to the cross. We remember what Jesus did for us and ask Him for the grace to humble ourselves and think of others, just as He did. We ask Him to give us the ability to see ourselves clearly and refocus our priorities on why we're in this race to begin with – to show the world that Jesus came to redeem us back to perfect unity with our Creator. And that's worth giving up our rights every day.

Romans 12:1-3 – *Therefore I urge you, brethren, by the mercies of God, to present your bodies a living and holy sacrifice, acceptable to God, which is your spiritual service of worship. And do not be conformed to this world, but be transformed by the renewing of your mind, so that you may prove what the will of God is, that which is good and acceptable and perfect. For through the grace given to me I say to everyone among you not to think more highly of himself than he ought to think; but to think so as to have sound judgment, as God has allotted to each a measure of faith.*

Making It Personal

How much do you think about imitating Christ? Is it important to you? Are there places in your heart where you have too high an opinion of yourself? Ask God to reveal any blind spots in your heart and mind and surrender anything that keeps you from imitating Christ.

Pray Today

Dear Jesus, We know that we can never imitate You in our own strength. Our hearts and minds must be transformed by Your Spirit, and this happens as we daily surrender to Your conviction, as a living sacrifice. Help us to be sensitive to others, and to see our brothers and sisters with the same eyes of compassion and love that You saw us. Teach us to make unity a priority, as we imitate the sacrifice You made on the cross on our behalf. Amen.

Day 13: Remember Who You Work For

For this reason also, God highly exalted Him, and bestowed on Him
the name which is above every name, so that at the name of Jesus
every knee will bow, of those who are in heaven and on earth and under the earth,
and that every tongue will confess that Jesus Christ is Lord,
to the glory of God the Father.
Philippians 2:9-11

When my daughters were in high school, they attended a classical Christian private school. It was very challenging academically, and the school placed great emphasis on getting accepted to college. Naturally, the students who excelled and won entrance to more prestigious universities were put forth as examples of what one could accomplish if you worked hard enough. Every spring, the high school graduation ceremonies focused on these high achievers. Each student's name was listed in the program, along with the college or university they would be attending. You can imagine the pressure this put on the average student. *No one* wanted their name listed under the local community college.

Our world puts a lot of emphasis on achieving success by working for the right people, attending the right schools, and becoming well-known. Simply being associated with the right organization can open doors of opportunity. We are all prone to need validation and it feels good to us to know that we are part of something big or valuable.

As a Christ-follower, we know the truth. There is nothing good in us, and any value we have comes entirely from our association with Jesus. Our filthy rags of self-righteousness have been exchanged for His robes of righteousness. We are adopted as children of God, co-heirs with Jesus. We are the promised bride of Christ, awaiting our bridegroom. It's all a gift, nothing we've earned.

But think about it...

We serve at the pleasure of the Creator of the universe.
We speak for the One who spoke the worlds into existence.
We are family to the One before whom every knee will bow.
We carry the name that is above every name.

Because we work for Jesus!

What organization has more influence and opportunity to change the world, than the kingdom of God? What business has more wealth and resources than the God who created everything that exists, and calls things into existence from nothing? What scientific think-tank has more knowledge than an omniscient Creator? What psychological group has more insight than the God who knows the thoughts and intents of the human heart?

Who do you work for? (Oh yes, let me tell you about my boss! Can I tell you my company's mission statement?)

Because our enemy has created a culture that makes Christianity look foolish and weak; because society has normalized sin as a civil right; because social media has made it politically incorrect to believe in absolute truth, we sometimes forget who it is we are serving. We represent the highest authority known to man. We hold the secrets of the universe in our hearts. We have the privilege and the responsibility and the authority to carry the gospel of Jesus Christ, the One whom God highly exalted.

One day, every knee will bow and confess that Jesus Christ is Lord. The fact that we serve Him now should not puff us up as though we have somehow earned this special privilege. Instead, it should fill us with humility and gratitude, and impress on us the urgency of sharing the good news with those who do not know Him.

But don't miss the joy and reality...you serve a great King. Your mission is backed by the resources and wealth of the Creator. You never need to be ashamed of who you work for. So, go tell the world.

Isaiah 45:5-6 – *I am the Lord, and there is no other; besides Me there is no God. I will gird you, though you have not known Me; that men may know from the rising to the setting of the sun that there is no one besides Me. I am the Lord, and there is no other.*

Making It Personal

Have you ever felt like you should apologize for your beliefs? Has the world made you feel foolish? Make a list of who God is from scripture to remind yourself who it is you are working for. Would you trade jobs with anyone?

Pray Today

Dear Jesus, How quickly we forget who You really are! We listen to the chatter of the unbelieving world, and somehow think we need to apologize for standing on Your Word and believing in You. How foolish! You are the One who is highly exalted, the name above every name. We are so thankful that You gave us the privilege of bowing our knees in this life and confessing that You are Lord. May we be faithful and proud to proclaim Your name to the unbelieving world around us. Forgive us for imagining You to be less than You truly are. Amen.

Day 14: No Whining Allowed

*Do all things without grumbling or disputing;
so that you will prove yourselves to be blameless and innocent,
children of God above reproach in the midst of a crooked and perverse generation,
among whom you appear as lights in the world.*
Philippians 2:14-15

"A house divided cannot stand."

Abraham Lincoln made that line famous in his 1858 speech while running for the U.S. Senate. It wasn't his original thought; he got it from Jesus. "Any kingdom divided against itself is laid waste; and any city or house divided against itself will not stand" (Matthew 12:25).

Paul's words about the effects of grumbling and disputing remind us of Jesus' warning. Just what does it mean to grumble or dispute, and why was Paul concerned about it? Does it really affect our kingdom work?

To grumble is more than just to complain. Sometimes complaints are necessary; if something is amiss or wrong, it can be valuable to bring it to the attention of the person responsible. However, the Greek word translated as *grumbling* (murmuring) has the idea of secrecy, or a displeasure not openly avowed.[1] We grumble when we share our discontentment with others, but not with the intent of a solution. We just want to be right, and have our unhappiness validated. *Disputing* is better translated as doubting. It is deliberating within our own thoughts, questioning what is true, mulling over things in our own mind.

Can you see how these two words (grumbling and disputing) work together to destroy our unity and effectiveness as a witness to the power of Christ? Something happens that annoys us or that we disagree with. We spend a few hours, or days, or weeks, cherishing these disgruntled thoughts, sharing them only with people we know will agree with us. Our words and attitudes cause division, leading others to think badly of our teammates, or fellow believers. The outcome is that the unbelieving world notices our grumbling and muttering and concludes that we are no different than they are. The light of Christ that should be shining in our lives is dimmed, obscured by our discontent.

Paul encourages us to set aside our grumbling so that we will become blameless (no accusation or blame "sticks" to us), and innocent (harmless or pure, free from evil and choosing only what glorifies God). While he recognizes that things will happen that we may dislike or disagree with, he reminds us that how we handle them has a huge impact on our ability to influence a crooked and perverse world.

Jesus gave us clear instructions on how to handle disagreements in Matthew 18. We are to go directly (and only) to the people involved. We are to be people who readily forgive (Ephesians 4:32, Matthew 6:14-15), avoid speculations that lead to arguments (2 Timothy 2:23-24), and choose rather to be wronged than to avenge ourselves at the expense of our testimony and the gospel (Matthew 5:11,39).

Choosing not to grumble and complain is not easy. It is our human tendency. But stepping back and giving thought to the damage it can do, not only to our relationships with each other and our fellowship with God, but also to the cause of Christ, enables us to make the better choice.

1 Corinthians 10:9-11 – *Nor let us try the Lord, as some of them did, and were destroyed by the serpents. Nor grumble, as some of them did, and were destroyed by the destroyer. Now these things happened to them as an example, and they were written for our instruction, upon whom the ends of the ages have come.*

Making It Personal

Do you have a tendency to grumble, sharing your discontentment with others? Has something caused you to doubt or question? If so, confess it as sin and ask God to help you deal with issues directly.

Pray Today

Dear Jesus, In our day, we express our opinions readily. We tweet them, post them on Facebook, and share them on social media. We want validation for our discontent, and You tell us clearly in Your Word that this is sin. We confess our murmuring and ask Your forgiveness. Remind us of the impact of our words and attitudes. Help us to remember that the world is watching, and we are to shine as lights in the darkness, giving an accurate picture of Your power in our lives. Teach us to set aside our petty disagreements and pursue peace with our brothers and sisters, so that the gospel is clearly seen. Amen.

Day 15: Don't Run In Vain

...holding fast the word of life,
so that in the day of Christ I will have reason to glory
because I did not run in vain nor toil in vain.
Philippians 2:16

This verse is a continuation of the preceding thoughts. Paul has urged us to set aside grumbling so that we offer no hindrance to the light of Christ that should shine through our lives into the dark world. We are to let go of *our* thoughts and words, and instead cling tightly to the word of life. This is what we offer the world as light.

The Greek word used here for "holding fast" means to put forth or present what we hold or possess.[1] We must have a firm grasp on God's Word and the gospel if we are going to present it to an unbelieving world. This is important to Paul. He has investment in the Philippian believers. He has taught them doctrine and theology and truth. He has corrected them. He has risked his life to preach the gospel to them. He did not want to come to the end of his life and realize all of it had been in vain, because they did not hold onto the word of life or understand the gospel fully.

To run in vain is for our work to be empty, fruitless. It is to have no lasting effect. It is to be devoid of truth. It is to spend our time, energy and resources on something that doesn't last.

Paul knew that the power of his ministry was not in his abilities or expertise, but in the word of God, the gospel that he proclaimed. He was passionate that the gospel he preached was the true gospel, with no imitations or substitutions.

How can we make sure that our race is not in vain? Here are three ways we hold fast to the word of life.

#1 – Hold fast to grace.

In his letter to the Galatians, Paul confronts the believers who are allowing distortions of the gospel by placing the Jewish believers under the yoke of the Law. He was adamant that they remain true and faithful to the message of salvation by grace, through faith, *since by the works of the Law no flesh will be justified* (Galatians 2:16). Paul knew personally how easy it would be to revert to a works-righteousness mentality; even Peter and Barnabas were caught up in this wrong teaching (Galatians 2:11-14). Salvation is a gift of God's grace, and good works are a result, and not the means, of redemption.

#2 – **Hold fast to Christ.**

In his letter to the Colossians, Paul confronts the believers who are being led astray by heretical teaching. The issues he addresses relate to the supremacy of Christ and the adequacy of the cross for salvation. In addition, he reminds the believers that all true knowledge is found in Christ. All things were created through Him and for Him; He is before all things; in Him all things hold together; in Him all the fullness of the deity of God dwelled in bodily form; in Him we are made complete. Paul warns us not to be defrauded by visions and fleshly ideas, taken captive by philosophy and empty traditions of men. Christ is enough, and He is everything.

#3 – **Hold fast to your faith.**

In his letter to the Thessalonians, Paul worries that the extreme suffering and persecution he is enduring will cause the believers to fall away from their faith, tempted by the enemy to grow discouraged. He sent Timothy to check on them and rejoices to hear that they are standing firm in faith and love, and that his work has not been in vain. He encourages them with the promise of the resurrection for those who have died, and the hope of the return of Jesus, which could happen at any moment. We hold fast to our faith, standing firm against temptation, and fully convinced in the future promises of God, despite suffering.

The word of life is all we have to offer. We are saved by grace. We are made complete, righteous and holy, in Christ alone. We stand firm in our faith, never allowing discouragement to cause us to stumble or fall away. Any other message is empty and vain.

2 Corinthians 6:1 – *And working together with Him, we also urge you not to receive the grace of God in vain—for He says, "At the acceptable time I listened to you, and on the day of salvation I helped you." Behold, now is "the acceptable time," behold, now is "the day of salvation"—giving no cause for offense in anything, so that the ministry will not be discredited.*

Making It Personal

How firm is your grasp on the gospel? Do you recognize distortions of the truth? What do you need to affirm in your understanding of scripture, so your race is not in vain?

Pray Today

Dear Jesus, How great a treasure You have placed in our hands – the gospel, the word of life. Help us hold fast to the truth, and be faithful to communicate it completely and effectively, so that our race is not in vain. Teach us to stand firm, complete in You, and proclaim the message of grace to all who will believe. Amen.

# Day 16: Be Poured Out

> *But even if I am being poured out as a drink offering*
> *upon the sacrifice and service of your faith,*
> *I rejoice and share my joy with you all. You too, I urge you,*
> *rejoice in the same way and share your joy with me.*
> Philippians 2:17-18

What a vivid example! Paul takes his readers back to the Old Testament practice of the drink offering, which was offered as an accompaniment to other offerings. He recognizes the sacrifice that others were making to remain faithful to Christ, and considers his own life as being poured out on their sacrifice. As a cup upturned, emptied completely, he was willing to give everything he had for people to come to know and believe in Christ, and to follow Him faithfully.

In the verses just following this statement (Philippians 2:19-30), Paul mentions two of the men who served alongside him, commending them both for their sacrificial service to the body. The younger convert, Timothy, whom Paul considered a son in the Lord, and Epaphroditus, his "fellow worker and fellow soldier" who served Paul by taking messages back and forth from the churches and ministered to Paul's needs. Like Paul, their lives were poured out, holding nothing back.

Each of these three men teach us something about what it means to live a life that is poured out for others and for the gospel.

#1 – Paul teaches us that a life poured out results in genuine joy in seeing people come to Christ and grow spiritually.

Giving up your life for the gospel will adjust your **perspective**. Yes, we still enjoy this life. Time spent with family is precious. Relaxing with friends, enjoying recreational activities, and allowing time to pursue hobbies is good and profitable for our physical and mental health. Traveling the world expands our appreciation for the beauty and diversity of the world God has created. But when God calls you to pour out your life, nothing quite satisfies you or brings you soul-satisfying joy like being part of another person's faith journey toward Christ.

#2 – Timothy teaches us that a life poured out results in genuine concern for others' welfare.

Giving up your life for the gospel will adjust your **priorities**. Paul genuinely wanted to know how the Philippian believers were doing. This was not a surface relationship. He wanted to know what was going on in their lives so he could address any issues, correct any teaching, and know how to pray specifically for them. So, he sent someone who had a "kindred spirit," the same heart of genuine concern. Pouring out your life means that your own interests are set aside in favor of meeting the needs of your fellow brothers and sisters in the body of Christ.

#3 – Epaphroditus teaches us that a life poured out results in genuine sacrifice to finish the task.

Giving up your life for the gospel will adjust your **passion**. Epaphroditus was a dedicated servant. Paul calls him a *worker*, a *soldier*, a *messenger*, and a *minister*, describing a man who was committed to the task. So much so, that he came close to death, risking his life to do what needed to be done in helping Paul carry the gospel to the Gentiles. We live, pouring out our lives, all the while being willing to be completely poured out. As Paul has said earlier in his letter, "To live is Christ, to die is gain."

Paul, Timothy, and Epaphroditus are imperfect examples of the perfect life poured out. As Jesus celebrated Passover with His disciples on the night before He went to the cross, he shared the cup, telling them, "This is My blood of the covenant, which is **poured out** for many for forgiveness of sins."

He endured the cross for the *joy* set before Him (Hebrews 12:2).
He set aside His glory in *concern for our welfare* (Philippians 2:5-7).
He finished the task, offering Himself as our *sacrifice* (Hebrews 10:12).
Jesus gives us the ultimate example of what it means to pour out your life. When we think of what it cost Him, what could we possibly have that would be worth holding back, or holding onto?

2 Corinthians 12:15 – *I will most gladly spend and be expended for your souls. If I love you more, am I to be loved less?*

Making It Personal

Are you willing to pour out your life for the gospel? Is there anything (or anyone) you would be unwilling to let go of, if God asked you to set it aside? Ask God to examine your perspective, your priorities, and your passion, and help you surrender anything you are holding too tightly.

Pray Today

Dear Jesus, You set the greatest example when You poured out Your life's blood on the cross. You held nothing back but gave all of Yourself for us. We want to bring You joy by giving back to You this life that You have blessed us with. Teach us to find our passion and purpose only in what matters for eternity. Let us be poured out for the sake of the kingdom, for the spread of the gospel to the world. Amen.

Day 17: Learn and Live

Finally, my brethren, rejoice in the Lord.
To write the same things again is no trouble to me, and it is a safeguard for you.
Beware of the dogs, beware of the evil workers,
beware of the false circumcision; for we are the true circumcision,
who worship in the Spirit of God and glory in Christ Jesus
and put no confidence in the flesh.
Philippians 3:1-3

I'm sure you're familiar with the saying, "live and learn!" We say it when we make a foolish mistake and suffer the consequences. It describes education gained by surprise, through personal experience.

Paul turns this phrase on its head. He likes to repeat himself because he wants the Philippian believers to learn, so they can live. Some knowledge is better gained by hearing the truth, rather than living with the scars of a lack of knowledge. In this case, he is warning about false teachers.

Hear this. The world is filled with false teachers, and in your journey to make Christ known, you will face many of them. Paul gives us three descriptions which help us identify those whose theology will lead us away from the true gospel of Christ.

The term "dog" was often used by the Jews to describe the Gentiles, whom they considered ceremonially impure or unclean. It describes those of moral impurity, who will be excluded from heaven (Revelation 22:15) and described male prostitutes in the Old Testament (Deuteronomy 23:18). A person who accepts and participates in immoral lifestyles (homosexuality, sex outside of marriage, and the many other perversions we see in our culture), yet claims to be in Christ, would fall in this category.

"Evil workers" are those who labor for wrong, wicked or destructive things; it describes false teachers who disguise themselves as Christ-followers. In our culture, the popular "prosperity gospel" would fall under this label. To present the gospel as a means of gaining physical, worldly success is a lie, leading many people to put their trust in a false hope, and obscuring the truth that is found in Jesus.

Many times, Paul met Jewish believers who wanted to place themselves and others under the Law of Moses as a requirement for salvation. By referring to this as the "false circumcision" he is speaking of the physical circumcision of the old covenant, which has no spiritual value. There are many false religions that are simply a works-based strategy for a hoped-for salvation (Islam, Hinduism, etc.), as well as Christians who seek an outward holiness through legalism and tradition rather than the sanctification of the Holy Spirit by the grace of God.

Three times Paul stresses that we are to **beware** of these dangerous teachings. The word means *to see, to perceive, and to take heed.* We must have our eyes open. We cannot assume that everyone who names the name of Christ truly belongs to Him. We must know the Word of God ourselves, the authentic, true theology, so that when we are presented with a false gospel, we immediately recognize its fatal flaws. We must **safeguard** the precious gospel, and present it clearly, without apology, and in return, the gospel will safeguard our lives.

We must learn, and live.

Paul reminds us what true worship is. We worship in the Spirit of God. How good it is to know that God's Spirit will remind us and teach us truth. This happens as we spend time in His Word, with quiet hearts, listening and praying, studying and memorizing, and applying what He shows us.

We also glory in Christ Jesus. If you want to discern the truth about someone's theology, ask them what they believe about Jesus. If Jesus is anything less than the divine Son of God, the only way of salvation, who was crucified, buried and resurrected for the sins of the world, you can confidently reject the teaching.

Paul's words of warning encourage us to be humble learners, open to the Spirit's correction, and wary of the deception of the enemy. We are entrusted with the gospel. Let us not be foolish or careless with this treasure.

Acts 4:12 - *And there is salvation in no one else; for there is no other name under heaven that has been given among men by which we must be saved.*

Making It Personal

Do you know the Word of God well enough, so that you are quick to recognize false teaching or distortions of the gospel? How do you respond? Why is it important that we safeguard the truth? Are you believing anything that is not true?

Pray Today

Dear Jesus, You are the way, the truth, and the life. You are our firm and certain foundation, and Your story, the gospel message, is a precious trust that we must keep. We ask that Your Spirit show us any error that we may have accepted and correct us according to Your word. Let us be vigilant and wary of false teachers, knowing that their words lead only to death. Instead, may we be bearers of truth and light that leads to life. Amen.

Day 18: Let Go Of Self-Confidence

> *...although I myself might have confidence even in the flesh.
> If anyone else has a mind to put confidence in the flesh, I far more:
> circumcised the eighth day, of the nation of Israel, of the tribe of Benjamin,
> a Hebrew of Hebrews; as to the Law, a Pharisee; as to zeal, a persecutor of the
> church; as to the righteousness which is in the Law, found blameless.*
> Philippians 3:4-6

We began this journey with the realization that it's not about us. Like Paul, we want to set aside the pursuit of anything other than knowing Christ. This requires an accurate estimation of our own abilities.

The word translated as "confidence" comes from the Greek verb *peithō*, meaning to trust, to be persuaded, to have assurance. Paul says he neither *has* confidence in his flesh nor *puts* confidence in his flesh. He doesn't trust himself, his accomplishments, or his good works (past or present) as able to accomplish the eternal purposes to which God has called him.

He makes a good point when he says that he of all people has a reason to rely on his own abilities. He's accomplished a lot. He has impeccable breeding. He comes from the right family, had the right education, and has kept the Jewish Laws perfectly. His track record is exemplary. It would have been easy for him to look at himself and think that God chose him because of his abilities and goodness.

The religious world of that day, the Jewish Sanhedrin, placed great responsibility and confidence in Paul. He was acting with their authority when he pursued the death of those who were following Jesus. But when Paul had his eyes opened (literally), he saw himself as God saw him – a blasphemer, a persecutor and a violent aggressor acting in ignorant unbelief.

Paul knew that all his flesh could offer was destruction and separation from God, no matter who approved of him, or how good he looked in comparison to other people. That is why he did not trust himself. He was not persuaded to believe in his own abilities.

Picture this. Make a list of all your good qualities. Collect your trophies, certificates of award, and diplomas. Print out your Linked-In profile and compile statistics on your Instagram followers. Add a copy of a lengthy resume of all you have achieved in your career, and don't forget your genealogy report showing all the famous people in your family lineage. Now put all that into a nice box and bring it into God's throne room. Set it down in front of Him as what you can offer as evidence that He chose well when He saved you, and why you're capable of serving Him.

What will you do when He calls over the smallest angel and asks him to take out the trash?

Maybe that's a ridiculous example, but isn't it exactly what we do when we put our faith in our own abilities? When we set out to accomplish something God has called us to do, and find ourselves relying on our own talents, our own strength?

Instead, let's do what Paul did. Let's put all our confidence and trust in God's ability to empower us and equip us to do what He wants done. Let's lean on Him and stop thinking about how we can hold ourselves up. Just as we had no power to achieve salvation, we have no power to accomplish our sanctification or the good works that He has prepared for us to do. And here's the good news. Maybe you've got absolutely nothing to put in your box. The same truth still applies. God doesn't need anything, but He only asks for your faithful obedience and trust. He'll do the rest.

When you find yourself wondering how in the world you're going to be able to do this, give it up. Instead, trust in the God who keeps the world spinning to do it through you.

1 Timothy 1:12-14 – *I thank Christ Jesus our Lord, who has strengthened me, because He considered me faithful, putting me into service, even though I was formerly a blasphemer and a persecutor and a violent aggressor. Yet I was shown mercy because I acted ignorantly in unbelief; and the grace of our Lord was more than abundant, with the faith and love which are found in Christ Jesus.*

Making It Personal

Is there any part of your life where you are trusting in your own abilities? Have you come to the end of your own strength and self-confidence? Ask God to reveal any places where you are not fully trusting Him to do the work and renew your confidence in Him alone.

Pray Today

Dear Jesus, How grateful we are that You chose us, not because of what we have done or accomplished, but simply because of mercy and grace. We have no ability in our flesh to accomplish any spiritual good work. We recognize our dependence on Your Holy Spirit to do the work through us. Give us full confidence in You and convict us gently when we are trusting in ourselves. We want Your power, not ours, and for You to get all the glory for everything we do. Amen.

Day 19: Follow My Example

Brethren, join in following my example, and observe those who walk according to the pattern you have in us. For many walk, of whom I often told you, and now tell you even weeping, that they are enemies of the cross of Christ, whose end is destruction, whose god is their appetite, and whose glory is in their shame, who set their minds on earthly things.
Philippians 3:17-19

The things you have learned and received and heard and seen in me, practice these things, and the God of peace will be with you.
Philippians 4:9

We've all heard the saying, "Do as I say, not as I do." It's used when we recognize our inability to take our own advice and want to save others the hard lessons we've learned. Paul was of a different mind. He encouraged the believers to imitate him.

One might see that as arrogance, but we know that was not Paul's heart. He considered himself the chief of sinners. He struggled with his flesh the same as you and I do (Romans 7). He had places of weakness. But he could confidently say, "follow my example" because he faithfully pointed to Christ in every part of his life. That is the value of a true mentor.

Paul mentored many young believers, including Timothy, whom he considered a beloved son in the faith. He loved to encourage new believers as he met with churches on his missionary journeys. His letters are filled with instruction, doctrine, and correction, all designed to bring the readers to one simple conclusion: "Jesus is everything, and He's all you need. Follow Him." He could say "follow me," because he was following Christ.

What was Paul's pattern? What can we see in these verses that we can imitate in a practical way?

#1 – A commitment to the cross of Christ.
Paul was passionate to preach Jesus crucified as the only way of salvation. No other gods would do. He knew that trusting in anything or anyone else for the atonement of sin would keep people separated from God, destined for hell. He was so committed to the gospel message of the cross that he told the Galatians that even if he himself preached a different gospel he was to be accursed. We imitate Paul when we commit our lives to proclaiming the power of the cross to save.

#2 – A commitment to self-sacrifice.
What does it mean when Paul warns against those "whose appetite is their god?" The word for "appetite" literally means "belly" or "womb" but metaphorically can

relate to the heart of man, the seat of thought, feeling and choice. It's the place of nourishment. It's what fills us up. It's where we find our security. It's what feeds our soul. An unbeliever worships the filling of his belly – he wants his comfort, his food, his satisfaction, and that is what he pursues. In contrast, Paul has learned the secret of following Christ is a willingness to be in need or want of physical and earthly pleasures. We imitate Paul when we set aside our own needs in pursuit of spiritual food, just as Jesus told his disciples (John 4:32).

#3 – A commitment to holiness.
Paul warns against those whose "glory is in their shame, who set their minds on earthly things." This one is an easy one to understand. An unbeliever or a Christian who is not living in obedience to Christ is distracted by worldly things. They tolerate sin, even participating in it. Instead of a worldview framed by the truth of scripture, they accept the cultural norms, and take pride in their independence and "sophisticated" view of life. We imitate Paul when we humbly submit to the commands of Christ, pursuing holiness in our thoughts and actions.

As believers, we need strong examples to follow. We need mentors. We need older, wiser adults to walk alongside us and show us a life that is committed to the cross, to self-sacrifice, and to holiness. And in turn, we must become those examples to those following behind us.

Paul tells us how this mentoring takes place. We learn, we receive, we hear, we see, and then we practice. A life that follows Christ is a life that can be imitated.

1 Corinthians 4:14-16 – *I do not write these things to shame you, but to admonish you as my beloved children. For if you were to have countless tutors in Christ, yet you would not have many fathers, for in Christ Jesus I became your father through the gospel. Therefore I exhort you, be imitators of me.*

Making It Personal

Who are your mentors? Who are you following? Are they committed to the cross? Do they exhibit a life of self-sacrifice? Do they set an example of holiness? If not, stop following. Ask God to bring someone into your life that follows Christ completely. Then, determine to be that example for those who are following you.

Pray Today

Dear Jesus, How thankful we are that You set the ultimate example to follow. You honored Your Father in your submission to the cross, setting a pattern for us to follow. May we always follow You faithfully, committed to the gospel of the cross, being willing to sacrifice our physical needs for the better, spiritual riches, and devoted to holiness. We want our lives to be examples others can follow to find You. Amen.

Day 20: Look Toward Home

*For our citizenship is in heaven,
from which also we eagerly wait for a Savior, the Lord Jesus Christ;
who will transform the body of our humble state into conformity
with the body of His glory, by the exertion of the power that He has
even to subject all things to Himself.*
Philippians 3:20-21

Our daughter and son-in-law spent two years living in a foreign country. During this time, she had her purse stolen and had to report it to the police. She commented that when she pulled out her "blue" passport, she was suddenly taken directly to the people in charge, and they took her complaint a lot more seriously. The power of the blue passport was not in its color, but in what it stood for. It meant she possessed all the rights and authority and benefits of citizenship in the United States of America. Because the U.S. was a respected ally, she was treated respectfully. Her citizenship gained her a certain measure of privilege.

Do you realize you also hold a very powerful spiritual passport? As Christ-followers, we are not only citizens of the kingdom of God, we are blood-related to the King. We are co-heirs with the Son of God. We are members of the family, brothers and sisters with all the saints from all the ages. We are part of a very special group of citizens, with all the rights, authority and privileges that citizenship in God's kingdom offers!

When we travel the world, we are required to show our passport as we enter different countries. Very often we must purchase a visa giving us special permission to be there, for a limited amount of time, and with certain restrictions. The more you travel, the more you understand the concept and value of citizenship. You must abide by the laws of the country; you eat foods that are particular to that place; you may even wear different clothing in respect of the nationals.

But you're still not a citizen of that country, unless you revoke your previous citizenship and declare your allegiance to your new country. You're just visiting.

If you're traveling the world, you know how important your passport is. It's the one thing your leaders will stress over and over: Don't. Lose. Your. Passport. Why? Because it will get you home!

Paul reminds us that we are simply visitors here. Our citizenship is in heaven. That's our home. That's where we belong. We're simply on assignment to represent the kingdom of God until our Savior and King, Jesus Christ, comes to get us. And when we get home, we're no longer going to worry about any laws or customs or tourist attractions of this world. All of that will fade away, and we'll enjoy our full rights and privileges of citizenship in the kingdom of heaven. In fact, we'll be given new bodies that are designed to live forever – the same kind of body Jesus received when He rose from the grave.

Our passport is not a little blue book. Our passport is the Spirit of God that indwells us, that gives us eternal life, and is the guarantee of our citizenship. When He took up residence in your spirit at the moment of salvation, He declared you a citizen of heaven. He will get us home.

So today, when you feel tired or discouraged, or dismayed at the pain and sorrow that fills the world, or even when you are enjoying moments of time with your brothers and sisters in Christ, don't forget where you belong. This place is not supposed to feel like home, because it's not where your citizenship lies. You're just visiting until the assignment is over, and you get to go home.

Ephesians 2:19 – *So then you are no longer strangers and aliens, but you are fellow citizens with the saints, and are of God's household.*

Making It Personal

Does this world feel like home to you? If it does, perhaps you need to re-examine your citizenship papers and remember where you belong. Are you longing for heaven? That's a good sign you know who issued your passport. Take joy and hope in the fact that your home is secure, and that this journey is only a temporary assignment.

Pray Today

Dear Jesus, We long for home. Your word tells us that You have set eternity in our hearts, and once we know You, we realize that we won't be truly at home until we are with You forever. Until then, You have given us assignments. You want us to invite others into the kingdom, to become citizens of heaven too. Help us to be content and faithful while we wait joyfully and anticipate our entrance into the place we really belong. Amen.

Day 21: Help The Struggling

> *Therefore, my beloved brethren whom I long to see, my joy and my crown,*
> *in this way stand firm in the Lord, my beloved.*
> *I urge Euodia and I urge Syntyche to live in harmony in the Lord.*
> *Indeed, true companion, I ask you also to help these women*
> *who have shared my struggle in the cause of the gospel,*
> *together with Clement also and the rest of my fellow workers*
> *whose names are in the book of life.*
> Philippians 4:1-3

Paul had a soft spot for those who struggle. When we read about him in the book of Acts, we see him as a man who never backs down in the face of adversity. He endures beatings, climbs over walls at night to escape death, gets thrown in prison, is mocked by demons, and is often falsely accused. We never see him waver in his faith. He trusts God completely, in all circumstances, and obeys without question.

Yet, we know he had some of the same inner struggles as all of us. He wrestled with his fleshly desires (Romans 7). He implores God repeatedly to remove a humbling "thorn in the flesh" (2 Corinthians 12:8). He experienced discord in relationships, refusing to take Mark along on his second missionary journey, because he had deserted them on his first trip (Acts 15:36-40). Paul recognized his own weaknesses and he knew that the growth process toward spiritual maturity and victory over sin did not come without conflict. But he also knew the importance of helping each other get there.

Apparently Euodia and Syntyche were not getting along. These were Christian sisters, members of the church body there in Philippi, but something had happened that caused division between them. Paul speaks directly and individually to both of them, urging them to live in harmony in the Lord.

What is harmony? The phrase used here means "same mind."[1] Paul has talked much about our minds in this letter, of the need for our thoughts to be aligned with Christ's mind of sacrifice, to have a proper and humble estimation of ourselves, and to be united in our minds, striving together for the gospel. He urges these two women to set aside their differences in order to bring harmony into the church, but he also brings accountability to the other members to help them achieve this.

Sometimes we need our brothers and sisters to step in and mediate for us. We need a fresh perspective. We need time for our emotions to settle. We need objective solutions, wisdom from those who have experience.

I love that translators chose the word "harmony" in this verse. We need unity that is rooted in the gospel and the Word of God, but we can have harmony as we recognize and appreciate our differences, such as personality, talent, giftedness, background, and preferences. Harmony is best illustrated in music; an orchestra may be made up of many different instruments, all making a different sound, but because they are playing the same piece of music, it becomes something beautiful and impactful.

All of us struggle at times.
All of us need help at times.

Paul did not give up on people. He told them the truth without apology. He expected those who belonged to Christ to obey Him. He set a high standard of holy living and passion for the gospel, but he did it with encouragement and humility.

Listen to how he refers to his teammates in the gospel: *beloved brethren, my joy and crown, my beloved.* He truly loved the people he served alongside; they were family. When they struggled, he was compelled to reach out with a steady hand and a kind word, until they were able to stand firm in the Lord.

Romans 12:15-16 – *Rejoice with those who rejoice, and weep with those who weep. Be of the same mind toward one another; do not be haughty in mind, but associate with the lowly. Do not be wise in your own estimation.*

Making It Personal

Do you know others who are struggling? How can you reach out to encourage them? Are you struggling? Who has God put in your life that can help you walk through a challenging time? Ask God, and then act on it.

Pray Today

Dear Jesus, How thankful we are that You do not give up on us when we struggle in our faith. How good it is that You have placed us in a family, with brothers and sisters who can help us when we are weak. Teach us to look beyond the surface smiles of our friends and teammates. Make us sensitive to those around us who are hurting and give us insight on ways to encourage and build up others. And when we struggle ourselves, help us to be brave enough to ask for help. Amen.

Day 22: Find The Joy

Rejoice in the Lord always; again I will say, rejoice!
Philippians 4:4

It always amazes us when we see people who ought to be discouraged because of the circumstances of life, but instead are filled with optimism and joy. What enables a person to rise above the drudgery of hard days and live with a joyful outlook?

Paul says that we should always rejoice, but he includes a qualification. **We rejoice in the Lord.** On the surface, we may not see any reason for rejoicing, but when we look through the lens of "in the Lord" we are able to find the joy.

Running the race is difficult. Whether it's a race with a defined beginning and end for a specific purpose, or simply the race of life, there are days when it might seem impossible to find anything to rejoice about. That's when we need to look at Paul's example to find a reason for joy. After all, we are commanded to rejoice. Joy is not optional for the Christ-follower.

Paul gives us three reasons to rejoice in his letter to the Philippians.

#1 – Proclaiming Christ brings joy.

Philippians 1:18 - *What then? Only that in every way, whether in pretense or in truth, Christ is proclaimed; and in this I rejoice. Yes, and I will rejoice.*

Being imprisoned did not bring joy to Paul. He felt the same as you and I would feel about being held somewhere he didn't want to be, his freedom restricted, his rights violated, stripped of his comforts, hungry, tired, and cold. There was nothing about his physical circumstances that would warrant an undeniable surge of joy flowing through his soul. So, what caused it? The knowledge that Christ was being proclaimed, not just despite his circumstances, but because of them. He was so thrilled that Jesus' name was being broadcasted publicly as a result of his misfortune he didn't care about his own discomfort.

#2 – Seeing others grow spiritually brings joy.

Philippians 2:17-18 - *But even if I am being poured out as a drink offering upon the sacrifice and service of your faith, I rejoice and share my joy with you all. You too, I urge you, rejoice in the same way and share your joy with me.*

Paul delighted in being part of others' spiritual growth. He sacrificed his time, his energy, his money, and his life to see the church expand and believers mature. He was so grateful to be used by God to advance the kingdom, his own circumstances didn't matter. Discomfort, even to the point of death, was a privilege if it meant that the people he loved and served learned what it meant to serve and obey God.

#3 – Meeting needs brings joy.

Philippians 4:10 - *But I rejoiced in the Lord greatly, that now at last you have revived your concern for me; indeed, you were concerned before, but you lacked opportunity.*

God's economy is different. The world says we must be independent and make our own success. But God teaches us to be dependent on one another in the body of Christ. It brings joy to us when we are used to meet needs, and it brings joy to us when we see God provide for us through those who meet our needs. We experience the love of God in tangible ways when we show concern for others, and this brings a deep, abiding sense of joy and satisfaction.

These are just three simple ways Paul had learned to rejoice. But all of them are meaningful because they operate "in the Lord." It is the Lord's name we proclaim. It is faith in the Lord that grows to maturity. And we serve as the Lord's hands and feet when we meet needs. We proclaim and grow and serve and share because we want people to know how our good God, the God who alone gives the true joy found in salvation. And that's a reason to rejoice.

Romans 12:10-13 – *Be devoted to one another in brotherly love; give preference to one another in honor; not lagging behind in diligence, fervent in spirit, serving the Lord; rejoicing in hope, persevering in tribulation, devoted to prayer, contributing to the needs of the saints, practicing hospitality.*

Making It Personal

What brings joy to you? Are there any circumstances in your life today that are causing you to be discouraged? How can you look at those circumstances through the lens of the gospel and find joy in them?

Pray Today

Dear Jesus, Life is hard sometimes. The circumstances of our lives are not always pleasant; in fact, there are days we'd like to give up. And we are often prone to complain and be discouraged. Teach us to find the joy. Help us look at every situation through Your eyes. Remind us to proclaim Your name. Help us to focus on others more than ourselves, encouraging their spiritual growth. And make us generous with our time, our energy, and our resources so that we can find the joy in meeting needs. We want to be filled with Your joy, so that others will see the difference You have made in our lives. Amen.

Day 23: Know That Jesus Is Near

Let your gentle spirit be known to all men. The Lord is near.
Philippians 4:5

This little verse has a great message for us, simply by its placement in scripture. Consider this: Philippians 4:4 speaks of joy, whereas verses 6-7 speak of peace. What does this tell us? A gentle spirit that testifies of the presence of Christ is found in the midst of joy and peace.

A "gentle spirit" is defined as forbearance, graciousness, moderation. It is a reasonableness, a considerate attitude that is kind and patient. Paul tells us this is the kind of attitude we are to have toward all men, no matter their spiritual condition, because Jesus is very close; He is near.

There are two ways to look at what Paul meant when he said, "The Lord is near." Because the early church fully believed that Christ could return at any moment, we can most likely assume that Paul meant this literally. Jesus' return is at hand; He is "near" in relation to time.

How would our words and actions change if we knew that tomorrow we would meet Jesus face to face? And not only us, but the people we love, the people we've been praying for? What would we want to say to them? How would we act toward them? If we knew the last thing we said to them **really was the last thing we would ever say to them?**

The Lord is near. Those words should cause a sense of urgency in us, to be clear about the gospel, and to use gentle and grace-filled words that draw others toward Christ.

We can also read this as Jesus is "near" in relation to place. His Spirit indwells us, and He is always near us. As Christ-followers, we are continually in the presence of Jesus.

What a difference it would make in our words, our attitudes, and our actions if we lived in a constant state of awareness of the presence of Jesus. First, we would experience the joy and peace that He desires for us to have. Second, how closely we would guard our thoughts and words. We would only say things that we know would please and honor Him. And third, we would carefully consider where we might go, what we read, what we listen to, and the things we participate in.

Would we be comfortable knowing Jesus was right beside us? Truly, the Lord is near.

No one likes to be around bitter, unhappy people. We've all probably experienced the awkwardness of being caught in family drama or walked into the middle of a heated conversation that doesn't involve us. What's our first instinct? Turn around and run! But the opposite is also true. When we meet someone that exhibits the joy and peace found in the presence of Christ, we are drawn to them. We want to be there.

This is the life that Paul is describing. Our words of grace and gentleness can draw people to Christ. A joy-filled heart and a peaceful attitude expressed in consideration and kindness invites others in, where we have an opportunity to tell them, "the Lord is near."

Are you full of joy?
Are you at peace?

Then let your gentle spirit be known to all men, for the Lord is nigh; He is at the door.

Colossians 4:5-6 – *Conduct yourselves with wisdom toward outsiders, making the most of the opportunity. Let your speech always be with grace, as though seasoned with salt, so that you will know how you should respond to each person.*

Making It Personal

What was the last thing you said? Was it gentle? Kind? Would it draw people toward Christ, or turn them away? How can you learn to walk in the awareness of the presence of Jesus?

Pray Today

Dear Jesus, We know that You are always with us. But because You are Spirit and we are flesh, sometimes we forget. Help us to be aware that You are near, and that You are returning soon. Show us how to be gracious and gentle to everyone we meet, so that they sense the joy and peace that comes from Your presence. We want others to be drawn to you. Amen.

Day 24: Anxiety Has An Answer

*Be anxious for nothing,
but in everything by prayer and supplication with thanksgiving,
let your requests be made known to God.
And the peace of God, which surpasses all comprehension,
will guard your hearts and your minds in Christ Jesus.*
Philippians 4:6-7

A quick search on the internet will provide you with some staggering statistics about anxiety and its ugly step-sister, depression. Estimates are that 18% of adults in the U.S. suffer from anxiety disorders, and 25% of children age 13-18. Anxiety affects a person physically, mentally, emotionally and spiritually, and manifests itself in a variety of phobias and disorders.

What is the answer to this epidemic? The world offers therapy and medication, and a variety of alternative treatments. But the fact is, anxiety is a sign of a greater, spiritual problem. While modern medicine and psychology may temporarily resolve the symptoms, God's Word tells us how to find the solution.

Our instinct is to seek peace itself. We do everything in our power to eliminate any source of anxiety. But Paul's advice is counter-intuitive. The solution according to God is not to change everything about our lives that makes us anxious, but to bring those anxieties to the One who can deal with them. We are to come with a spirit of gratitude for what we do have and ask Him to provide what we need. Then, we leave it with Him.

How does this work practically? Here's an example. Maybe you're anxious about being able to accomplish a challenge that is in your path. You don't feel ready or that you will have the ability to perform what is necessary. Your stomach is in knots, and you can't sleep for thinking about it. Your instinct is to take the challenge off the table, believing that is the source of your anxiety. In reality, your anxiety comes from a lack of trust in God, who called you to this task. Instead of avoiding the challenge, you thank Him for the opportunity for His strength to be made perfect in you. You acknowledge your fear and ask Him to give you the strength and tenacity to be obedient. Your trust moves from yourself and your inability, to faith in Him and His ability. This brings a supernatural peace as you relinquish both control of the situation and the expected result.

This doesn't necessarily mean you won't fail in the challenge. But your heart and your mind will be at peace, whatever the outcome, because your faith has grown, and you've learned just a little bit more about trusting God and worrying less. And the next time you face a challenge, you'll remember His faithfulness and be quick to lay aside any anxiety in favor of a grateful heart that fully relies on Him.

Notice that the peace of God guards both your heart and your mind. You'll start to *feel* differently and *think* differently. Gratitude changes your perspective, causing you to feel differently about the situation. And prayer elevates God in your thoughts; you begin to focus less on yourself and more on who God is. You think differently when you realize how small your problems are in comparison to the greatness of God.

You may be thinking, "I've prayed about this, but I'm still anxious. It doesn't work for me." I would encourage you not to give up on God's prescription for anxiety. Just like an antibiotic takes time to work against an infection in your body, it takes time to learn to trust God.

That's why Paul's words are written in the present tense. It's an on-going practice. Every time you start to feel anxious, stop and pray. Find something to be grateful for in spite of what causes you to worry. And let the peace of God have its way in your heart and mind.

John 14:27 - *Peace I leave with you; My peace I give to you; not as the world gives do I give to you. Do not let your heart be troubled, nor let it be fearful.*

Making It Personal

What makes you anxious? What can you find to be grateful for in that situation? What do you need to ask God for, instead of worrying?

Pray Today

Dear Jesus, You tell us in Your word not to worry. You remind us that worry cannot accomplish anything, and that our Heavenly Father knows what we need before we ask Him. Help us to look at every challenge as an opportunity to be grateful. Teach us to rely on You, and let Your peace be the guardian of both our thoughts and our feelings. Amen.

Day 25: Mind Your Thoughts

Finally, brethren, whatever is true, whatever is honorable, whatever is right, whatever is pure, whatever is lovely, whatever is of good repute, if there is any excellence and if anything worthy of praise, dwell on these things.
Philippians 4:8

How powerful is your mind?

Consider what one science website had to say about the capability of the human brain, compared to a computer.

- *The brain is both hardware and software, whereas there is an inherent difference in computers. The same interconnected areas, linked by billions of neurons and perhaps trillions of glial cells, can perceive, interpret, store, analyze, and redistribute at the same time.*
- *The same calculations and processes that might take a computer a few million steps can be achieved by a few hundred neuron transmissions, requiring far less energy and performing at a far greater efficiency.*
- *Essentially, the human brain can rewire itself. Neurons can disconnect and reconnect with others, and even change in their basic features, something that a carefully constructed computer cannot do.*[2]

That last point is simply amazing. A computer can only do what it is programmed to do. It cannot "rewire" itself. Our minds, however, can be trained and taught to think differently. God created us in such a way that even our physical mind can be regenerated and renewed when we begin to think different thoughts.

A few years ago, I challenged myself to memorize passages of scripture. I was amazed at how my middle-aged mind was able to retain large portions over time, even complete books of the New Testament! I made the observation to a friend that it truly felt like that my brain was being "rewired," that there were new "grooves" in my thinking.

No wonder scripture talks so much about the mind. What goes into our minds through our senses and experiences has immeasurable impact on our worldview, our ability to function in society, and especially on our relationship with God.

We are what we think and believe.

Paul urges us to consider carefully what we think about. The word he uses for "think" is *logizomai*, meaning to reason or ponder, to weigh or meditate. Some translations use the word "dwell" giving us the picture of letting our minds "camp out" and take time to really contemplate.

We are to think about things that are…

True (what is absolute truth of scripture, not relative truth of culture)
Honorable (what is honest and noble, not deceitful)
Right (what is righteous, not evil or unrighteous)
Pure (what is holy, not perverted or wicked)
Lovely (what is acceptable and pleasing to God, not sinful or dirty)
Good Repute (what is good and gracious, not gossip or slander)
Excellent (what is virtuous, morally good, not immoral)
Worthy of Praise (what is commendable, not what should be hidden)

Of course, the primary source of these thoughts is scripture. God's Word passes inspection on every single category mentioned. Scripture also serves as the standard by which we measure every other thought that comes into our minds. We can dwell on these things through music that honors God and lifts our thoughts to praise, through books and media that fill our minds with truth and cause us to ponder about the goodness and greatness of our God. And we can choose to set aside any and all thoughts that are the opposite, whether it is the entertainment we consume, or the attitudes and thoughts of our hearts toward other people.

Paul tells us we have the mind of Christ (1 Corinthians 2:16). Our minds were once blinded by the enemy (2 Corinthians 4:4) and even now, as Christ-followers, our minds are susceptible to being led astray and deceived (2 Corinthians 11:3). We are instructed to take every thought captive, so that our minds are not raised up against the knowledge of God (2 Corinthians 10:5).

When we commit to setting our minds on what pleases God, we will discover real knowledge and wisdom. Only then will we be able to recognize the deceptive culture around us and have answers for those who are looking for the truth.

1 Peter 1:13 - *Therefore, prepare your minds for action, keep sober in spirit, fix your hope completely on the grace to be brought to you at the revelation of Jesus Christ.*

Making It Personal

What consumes your mind? Are you careful about what goes in? What do you need to change in your thinking?

Pray Today

Dear Jesus, Thank You for giving us the mind of Christ. Because Your Spirit indwells us, we are able to think thoughts worthy of You. Teach us to guard our minds and use this great gift of thought and reason to honor You and grow in our knowledge of You. We don't want to waste a single thought. Amen.

Day 26: Be Content

> *Not that I speak from want, for I have learned to be content in whatever circumstances I am. I know how to get along with humble means, and I also know how to live in prosperity; in any and every circumstance I have learned the secret of being filled and going hungry, both of having abundance and suffering need. I can do all things through Him who strengthens me.*
> Philippians 4:11-13

If I asked you to describe for me the picture of "contentment," what would you say? I imagine we all would have a different version, depending on our personal likes or dislikes. What would be more telling, however, is to ask you what makes you "discontent?" What disturbs the peace of your heart? What creates an unexplainable or unfulfilled longing? What gives you that vaguely dissatisfied feeling you can't quite put into words?

Wouldn't we all like to know Paul's secret of contentment?

The first thing we see is that contentment has nothing to do with our physical circumstances. Discontent can poke holes in our emotional well-being when we're enjoying a life of abundant provision and pleasure as easily as it does when we're suffering or in need. Paul has lived on both sides of the track, so to speak. He's enjoyed prosperity as well as humility, and he's had to learn contentment in both worlds. He's enjoyed having every need fulfilled, going to bed with a full stomach in a safe and comfortable place. He's also spent nights in jail, hungry for food and friendship. Whether life is good or bad has no bearing on his contented state of mind.

So, what's the secret? I believe it is two-fold.

#1 – Paul trusted in the strength of God.

The word "content" comes from the Greek word *autarkēs*, a compound word from *autos* (same or self) and *arkeō* (possessed of unfailing strength, suffice, sufficient).[1] Paul was content, because he possessed the strength necessary to experience life. His outlook did not depend on what was happening, because he possessed the inner strength and fortitude to remain undisturbed. He simply navigated through the circumstances with his heart and mind undistracted and devoted to the gospel, by a supernatural strength.

You see, that verse we love so much, "I can do all things through Him who strengthens me" is written in direct context to contentment. It was not Paul's self-sufficient strength. It was God's strength operating in him that gave him the ability to "get along" in every circumstance.

#2 – Paul trusted in the sovereignty of God.

What has Paul already told us in this letter to the Philippians? He is confident that God began a good work in him and would complete it (1:6). He is assured that the circumstances of his imprisonment have advanced the gospel (1:12). He is convinced that Christ will be exalted, even if he dies (1:20). He has no doubt that suffering is part of God's plan (1:29). He is certain that God is working in him and through him (2:13). He is sure that God chose him for a particular purpose (3:12). And he is resting in the knowledge that heaven is waiting when his journey is complete (3:20).

A firm grasp of God's sovereignty leads to contentment. It takes away any doubt that our circumstances are evidence that God has forgotten us or neglected to care for us. It assures us that He does, indeed, know every detail of what is going on in our lives and has a purpose for it. Trusting that God is sovereign elevates every event, every hardship, and every blessing as a way for God's glory to be seen and the gospel to be preached. It fills us with peace and contentment in a way that no physical circumstance can ever provide.

Paul had a great perspective on what life should be. He desired to spread the gospel. He desired to be a godly man. And he desired to teach and train new believers how to live with contentment. Towards the end of his life, he tells young Timothy, *We have brought nothing into the world, so we cannot take anything out of it either. If we have food and covering, with these we shall be content* (1 Timothy 6:7-8). What a great attitude to emulate as we seek to live our lives on mission for the gospel.

2 Corinthians 12:9-10 – *And He has said to me, "My grace is sufficient for you, for power is perfected in weakness." Most gladly, therefore, I will rather boast about my weaknesses, so that the power of Christ may dwell in me. Therefore I am well content with weaknesses, with insults, with distresses, with persecutions, with difficulties, for Christ's sake; for when I am weak, then I am strong."*

Making It Personal

What would you say is your level of contentment? How will you walk in God's strength today? How is He working out His sovereign plans in your life?

Pray Today

Dear Jesus, How confident we are in Your strength! How hopeful our lives are when we see them from the perspective of Your sovereignty. Teach us to be content. Show us how to lean into the strength Your indwelling Spirit provides and help us find true contentment, joy, and peace in every circumstance, knowing that it is designed to bring You glory and be a place where the gospel is shared. Amen.

Day 27: Live Generously

*Nevertheless, you have done well to share with me in my affliction.
You yourselves also know, Philippians, that at the first preaching of the gospel,
after I left Macedonia, no church shared with me in the matter of giving and
receiving but you alone; for even in Thessalonica you sent a gift more than once for
my needs. Not that I seek the gift itself, but I seek for the profit which increases to
your account. But I have received everything in full and have an abundance;
I am amply supplied, having received from Epaphroditus what you have sent,
a fragrant aroma, an acceptable sacrifice, well-pleasing to God.*
Philippians 4:14-18

Missions and money. The two are intertwined, often to our dismay. On the one hand, we have the one going, called by God to a specific place, for a specific time, to accomplish specific work for the kingdom of God. On the other hand, we have the giver, who possesses God-given resources that He multiplies to support the work He desires to do. But are these two mutually exclusive?

Paul's wise words encourage us that going *and* giving should be the pattern of life for all Christ-followers. He thanks the Philippians for their gifts for his support. They have provided for his physical needs, and their generosity has encouraged him. He makes no apology for needing support. In 1 Corinthians 9:14, we learn that Jesus approved a person called to proclaim the gospel to make their living from it (encouragement for all who must raise funds to support missional work).

Paul benefitted from the financial gifts of the Philippian believers, but he also wants them to know that the benefits they receive by giving. He is excited for them, because by their gifts, they are gaining "profit which increases to their account." What does he mean?

The word profit is better translated "fruit." The account he is speaking of is a heavenly account; more specifically, a heavenly *accounting*. All of us will stand before God and give account for our deeds on earth (Romans 14:12, 2 Corinthians 5:10). That accounting will include how we've used the gifts and resources we've been given, whether we have used them for our own comfort and pleasure, or for God's glory. By giving generously, the Philippians were bearing spiritual fruit, giving evidence of God's work in their own hearts. They were storing up treasures in heaven, just as Jesus taught us in His words in the Sermon on the Mount (Matthew 6:19-21). How they used their treasures revealed the condition of their hearts (*Where your treasure is, there your heart will be also.*)

Paul also gave generously himself. At times, he chose not to receive support, serving one congregation for free while depending on the blessings of other believers who were in a better position to give (2 Corinthians 11:7-9). He often worked as a tentmaker to provide his own needs, to be an example as a hard worker, and not to be a burden on anyone (2 Thessalonians 3:6-13, Acts 18:1-4). And he delighted in delivering the gifts of one congregation to the poor in another district (Galatians 2:10, Romans 15:26).

The biblical strategy of generous living is recognizing that everything we have is provided by God and is to be used for His kingdom purposes. We live generously when we give both our money, our time, and our talents. Our attitude should be that of open and willing hands, however God wants to use what He has graciously allowed us to steward. Whether you are on the field as a full-time missionary, serving with a short-term mission team, or simply learning to live "on mission" in your own neighborhood, the response is the same.

Give generously.
Live generously.

As God brings opportunities for you to share both your abilities and your possessions, be obedient and faithful to give. When we combine a generous spirit with a contented heart, we will truly offer up a sacrifice that is well-pleasing to God, a sweet smell that permeates heaven.

2 Corinthians 9:6-7 – *Now this I say, he who sows sparingly will also reap sparingly, and he who sows bountifully will also reap bountifully. Each one must do just as he has purposed in his heart, not grudgingly or under compulsion, for God loves a cheerful giver.*

Making It Personal

What resources, abilities, or talents has God given you to manage? Do you hold them with open hands? Do you have a generous heart? Ask God how He wants to use the blessings He's given you.

Pray Today

Dear Jesus, Nothing we possess is by our own doing. Whatever we have, whatever we can do, is only by Your grace and Your power. Our lives are a stewardship of grace and we want to manage them well for Your glory, and for Your kingdom. Teach us to be generous. Help us to see opportunities to give. When we get to heaven, we want to have a storeroom filled with treasures to lay at your feet in gratitude for what You have done for us. May our hearts be content with the spiritual abundance that comes from serving You, and may we find great joy and delight in giving generously for the sake of the gospel. Amen.

Day 28: God Always Provides

*And my God will supply all your needs
according to His riches in glory in Christ Jesus.*
Philippians 4:19

What could you possibly need that God isn't able to provide?

Paul is emphatic in his statement: God will supply **all** your needs. The word supply means "to fill to the top, to abound, to complete." There is never a lack, no matter how great the demand. Like the widow's jar of oil that kept on pouring until every vessel in the house (and all she could borrow) were filled and running over (2 Kings 4), God's supply doesn't stop until the need is met.

The story of Elisha and the widow with great need teaches us the same truth that Paul has just related in the previous verses. If we want our needs to be met, we must be willing to share what we've already been given. The empty vessels could not be filled until the widow had faith to pour out what little oil she possessed. Her single vessel simply became a conduit of God's abundant grace that saved her family.

God meets our needs according to ***His riches***. And all of those riches are found in Christ, both spiritual and physical. By definition, His riches imply abundance and plenty.

God is rich in kindness and patience (Romans 2:4).
God is rich in wisdom and knowledge (Romans 11:33).
God is rich in forgiveness (Ephesians 1:7).
God is rich in grace (Ephesians 2:7).
God is rich in strength (Ephesians 3:16).
God is rich in understanding (Colossians 2:2).

Which do you think is more difficult for God? To forgive your sins, or to pay your bills? What is more challenging for the Creator of all that exists? To secure your eternal salvation, or put food on your table?

Silly isn't it? Why do we worry about our physical needs if we have faith to trust God for the spiritual ones? Jesus reminds us that if God can clothe the lilies of the field more beautifully that Solomon in all his glory, and feed the sparrows who never plant a seed, then He is well able to take care of our needs (Matthew 6:25-34).

Does this mean that we can sit at home and wait for groceries to be dropped off on our doorstep? Does it imply that we can sleep in until noon and not bother going to work? Of course not. Listen to Paul's words to the Thessalonian believers. Apparently, some people were unwilling to work, living indolent, unruly, wasted lives.

For even when we were with you, we used to give you this order: if anyone is not willing to work, then he is not to eat, either. For we hear that some among you are leading an undisciplined life, doing no work at all, but acting like busybodies. Now such persons we command and exhort in the Lord Jesus Christ to work in quiet fashion and eat their own bread. (2 Thessalonians 3:10-12)

In other scriptures, we are admonished to labor with our hands, not just to meet our own needs but to share with others in need (Ephesians 4:28, Acts 20:35, 1 Thessalonians 4:11-12). We are to work heartily, as to the Lord, rather than for men (Colossians 3:23). Work is honorable and necessary. It's how the body of Christ accomplishes what God calls us to do.

We do our part in working hard at whatever God calls us to do. It's an act both of obedience and faith. We obey, and trust God to provide.

God promises many times in scripture to meet your needs, to take care of what is necessary for you to do the work that He has called you to do. As Jesus said, the Father knows what we need, and as we seek first His kingdom and His righteousness, all those things will be taken care of by our Father.

2 Corinthians 9:8 – *And God is able to make all grace abound to you, so that always having all sufficiency in everything, you may have an abundance for every good deed.*

Making It Personal

What are your needs? Are you struggling with faith to believe He can and will meet those needs? Make a list. Ask the Father to provide. Now, go do what He's called you to do and leave the results to Him.

Pray Today

Dear Jesus, Thank You for reassuring us that the Father knows what we need. He is trustworthy. He has never failed us. Help us to set aside our worries, because worry implies that we don't trust You. Give us the strength and wisdom to be faithful workers in Your kingdom, and trust that all our needs will be met, in God's time and in His ways. Amen.

Day 29: Forget The Past

Brethren, I do not regard myself as having laid hold of it yet; but one thing I do: forgetting what lies behind and reaching forward to what lies ahead...
Philippians 3:13

Paul's declaration that he is intentionally trying to forget the past is unusual, especially for a Jew. The Jewish faith is filled with remembrances. Altars that were built to stand as a testimony for future Jews. Traditions that were handed down for generations. Deuteronomy 4:9 admonished the Israelites to take heed that they "**do not forget** the things which your eyes have seen and they do not depart from your heart all the days of your life; but make them known to your sons and your grandsons." We are told many times in scripture to remember what God has done (Psalm 105:5, Psalm 143:5, Isaiah 46:9).

We never forget what *God* has done. We forget what *we* have done.

The context of Paul's forgetting is his desire to reach the goal of his life: to know Christ in all His power as he experienced a life of suffering because of his faith, and of being conformed to His image. He had learned that focusing on what lay behind him was not helpful, but actually hindered his progress. Here are three things we need to forget in order to reach forward to what lies ahead.

Forget your past life.
Jesus tells us in Luke 9:62 that "no one, after putting his hand to the plow and looking back, is fit for the kingdom of God." Picture a farmer, setting out behind his plow to create a long, straight furrow in which to plant. He fixes his eyes ahead so that with a gentle tug of the reins or a quiet word of encouragement, he can direct the oxen to pull straight towards the horizon. How would his row look if he kept glancing back over his shoulder? He would have the same result many of us do when we take our eyes off the road to gaze at some distraction – the wheel pulls to the side and we veer off the road, hopefully to catch ourselves before we wreck!

To be "fit" for the kingdom of God is to be useful, ready and well-placed.[1] Jesus isn't saying that you're simply not good enough for kingdom work if you happen to look back towards your old life, but that you're not ready to be used by Him for the plans He has for you. We look back when we start to think about what life was like before He called us. We look back when we begin to doubt if He really did, when it gets hard, or confusing. We look back when we our flesh longs to regain control of our lives because let's face it, following Jesus is a blessed path, but it's not an easy one.

Forget your past failures.
Our enemy has a great way of reminding us where we've failed. He's called the "accuser" for a reason. That's why Paul reminds us in Romans 8:1, *There is now no*

condemnation for those who are in Christ Jesus. Looking back at how many times you've failed God can stop you in your tracks and cause you to decide you're just not ready to move forward with the new work He has put in your heart. The enemy whispers cruel things to your heart, such as "Who do you think you are to share the gospel?" and "If people really knew who I know you to be, they would never want to listen to you or believe anything you say." God has promised to forget your failures, and to bury your sin in the deepest sea (Micah 7:19). The only thing He's reminding you of is His covenant love and mercy that covered them all. So, forget your past failures; they will only hold you back from the prize.

Forget your past accomplishments.
This one is probably harder than the first two. We like to remember the times in our lives when we have been successful. No one wants to forget the good times. And there's nothing wrong with celebrating what God has accomplished in and through you. Paul's point is that we should not be satisfied and think we can sit out the rest of the journey. There's more work to be done. There are more people who need Jesus. There are more brothers and sisters who need encouragement. There is still more work to be done in the body of Christ, where your giftedness is needed. And we are always in need of more of God's sanctifying work in our own hearts and minds.

Paul reminded us of this earlier in Philippians 1:6, that it is God *who began a good work in [us]*, and it is God who will *perfect it until the day of Christ Jesus.* Continually looking back at what *we've* accomplished allows pride to raise its ugly head in our hearts, instead of a spirit of humility and dependence on the Spirit of God to accomplish the work. The reality is, getting us to focus on our past accomplishments is just as much a strategy of our enemy as focusing on our failures. Don't fall for it.

Forget what lies behind and reach forward to what lies ahead. That's the only way to run the race.

1 Corinthians 9:24 – *Do you not know that those who run in a race all run but only one receives the prize? Run in such a way that you may win.*

Making It Personal

What do you need to forget?

Pray Today

Dear Jesus, During Your ministry, many people desired to follow You, but in the end, decided to turn back. We don't want to be those people. Teach us to keep our eyes focused on You, with our hearts fully devoted to the goal of knowing You. Help us to forget our old lives, our failures and our victories, and run faithfully today. Amen.

Day 30: Press On

*Not that I have already obtained it or have already become perfect,
but I press on so that I may lay hold of that for which also
I was laid hold of by Christ Jesus. ... I press on toward the goal
for the prize of the upward call of God in Christ Jesus.*
Philippians 3:12,14

What encouraging words. Christ has laid hold of Paul for a reason, and it is that reason that motivates and inspires and encourages Paul to keep on running the race. He is hungry to apprehend the prize. Think about that for a minute. Paul has taught us that there is nothing in life that compares with knowing Christ, and that he has been and is willing to give up everything in order to achieve that knowledge. What he is saying here is that **God laid hold of him** because **He wanted** Paul to know Christ. God was the *pursuer*. God was the *initiator*. God desired Paul to have intimate, life-changing, purposeful, and practical knowledge of His Son.

To "lay hold of" something is to apprehend, to seize upon, or to take possession of.[1] Those are powerful words when we think about what God did for us. He confronted us in our sin, convicted us by His Spirit, and wooed us with His grace. He granted us repentance and faith to believe. He is the *One who has shone in our hearts to give the Light of the knowledge of the glory of God in the face of Christ* (2 Corinthians 4:6).

Now, in response to that heart- and eye-opening experience, we hunger for more of the knowledge of Christ. What began our relationship with Christ (the initial knowledge of Him) fuels our journey with Christ (a hunger for more knowledge of Him).

That is the prize.

Paul says that he will **press on.** To press on means to pursue, to run swiftly so as to reach the goal, to run or seek after eagerly. It is an earnest endeavor.[1]

To press on takes effort.
To press on takes dedication.
To press on take stamina.
To press on takes devotion.

Paul is telling us in no uncertain terms: I. Will. Not. Give. Up.

Of course, he has no strength to press on without the strength of the Spirit of God who lives in him and empowers him. If Paul runs in his own human flesh, by his own efforts, he will fail. And indeed, if you look at Paul with human eyes, you might think he's failing already.

He's in prison. He's growing old. He has trouble seeing. His body is wearing out. He owns nothing. He is dependent on the generosity of others to live.

But oh, if we look at Paul with spiritual eyes, we see that he is nearing the finish line. Suffering for the cause of Christ has worn off the rough edges of his personality and his heart is tender towards the believers. He's experienced the power of Christ in miraculous ways. He walks in close fellowship with the Spirit, his very steps directed by God's still, small voice. He's unafraid no matter who he stands in front of, always ready to speak the gospel. His sees people with the eyes of Christ; he teaches and corrects with the wisdom of Christ; he writes to the churches with the compassion of Christ.

He is nearing the goal, and his eyes are on the prize.

Paul doesn't know it, but in just a few short years, his race will be complete. His life will end in a Roman prison, a martyr for his faith. As he wrote to Timothy in his last letter, he will have *fought the good fight, finished the course, and kept the faith* (2 Timothy 4:7).

What would Paul tell us, if we could talk to him today? I believe he would say the same thing he's been saying throughout this little letter to the Philippian church.

Keep your eyes on the prize of knowing Christ.
Let God do the work in you first, and then watch as He works through you to accomplish the plans He made for your life before time began.

And don't forget, dear one, **press on**.

2 Corinthians 4:16-17 – *Therefore we do not lose heart, but though our outer man is decaying, yet our inner man is being renewed day by day. For momentary, light affliction is producing for us an eternal weight of glory far beyond all comparison.*

Making It Personal

Are you ready to give up, or are you pressing on? Is there something that needs to change in your pursuit of the prize?

Pray Today

Dear Jesus, Thank You for taking hold of us! We can't wait until we know You in fullness, face to face. What a glorious future we have in You. Until then, keep our hearts faithful, our eyes fixed on You, and our minds fully devoted as we grow in our knowledge of You. Help us to press on, as faithful servants like Paul, until our race is complete. We love You. Amen.

A Final Word

Our hope is that you have been blessed by this devotional and encouraged as you run the race that God has set before you. If you are a believer, go and proclaim the gospel, so that God's glory will be seen. If you are not a believer, here is how you can respond to Christ's invitation of salvation, by grace.

Believe that God created you for a relationship with Him.
Genesis 1:27 – *God created man in His own image, in the image of God He created him; male and female He created them.*
Colossians 1:16 – *All things have been created through Him and for Him.*

Recognize that you are separated from God.
Romans 3:23 - *For all have sinned and come short of the glory of God.*

Be willing to turn from your sin and repent.
1 John 1:9 – *If we confess our sins, He is faithful and righteous to forgive us our sins and to cleanse us from all unrighteousness.*

Acknowledge that Jesus died on the cross and rose from the grave.
Romans 10:9-10 – *That if you confess with your mouth Jesus as Lord, and believe in your heart that God raised Him from the dead; you will be saved; for with the heart a person believes, resulting in righteousness, and with the mouth he confesses, resulting in salvation.*

Invite Jesus in to control your life through the Holy Spirit.
John 1:12 – *But as many as received Him, to them He gave the right to become children of God, even to those who believe in His name.*

What To Pray

Dear Jesus, I recognize that I am separated from You because of my personal sin, and I need Your forgiveness. I believe that You died on the cross to pay the penalty for my sin. I confess my sin and ask You to forgive me. By faith, I turn from my way of life to follow You instead and accept Your gift of salvation by grace. I ask You to come into my life and transform me. Thank You for saving me and giving me eternal life. Amen.

If you sincerely prayed this prayer and surrendered your life to God, you are now His child. Please share this decision with another believer and ask him or her to help you get started in how to walk in your new life in Christ. We would love to hear about your decision!

Available Resources

AroundTheCornerMinistries.org

Going Around The Corner Bible Study
ISBN: 9780692781999 / List Price: $12.99
This six-session workbook helps believers explore the mission field in their own neighborhood and workplace. Learn to engage others through prayer and biblical good works guided by the prompts of the Holy Spirit. Gain confidence to evangelize through sharing the complete gospel and your own story and discover how to establish and equip new believers in their faith. A simple, practical and biblical strategy for disciple-making.

Going Around The Corner Bible Study, Student Edition
ISBN: 9780692781999 / List Price: $10.99
A five-session workbook covering the first four chapters of the original study for high school and college students with expanded commentary and practical application, focusing on reaching their campus, dorm, and playing field for Christ. Students will be guided into God's Word and develop an awareness and passion for sharing the gospel.

Going Around The Corner Bible Study, Leader Guide
ISBN: 9780999131824
List Price: $3.99
Key truths for each week, helpful discussion starters and thoughtful questions to help your group apply the principles in the study, plus suggested group activities and practical application steps. Adaptable for use with the Student Edition.

40 Days of Spiritual Awareness
ISBN: 9780999131800 / List Price: $9.99
A 40-day devotional to understand who God is and how He is working in the people right around you. Each day discover truth that will increase your awareness of God, yourself, other believers, and unbelievers. Be reminded of what is important: an awareness of God's work in our world, as He redeems and saves. At the end of the journey, you will realize that you are an important part of accomplishing that work and be prepared to join Him.

Living In Light of the Manger
ISBN: 9780999131817 / List Price $9.99
If the manger only has meaning during our holiday celebrations, we've missed the point of the story. Jesus was born, so that we could be *born again*. The events of His birth and the people who welcomed Him have many lessons to teach us about the glorious gospel and how Jesus came to change our lives. Discover the purpose and power of the manger through 40 daily devotions. Perfect to introduce the gospel to friends, co-workers and neighbors.

Grace & Glory: A 50-Day Journey In The Purpose & Plan Of God
ISBN: 9780999131848 / List Price $11.99
What do we do when we face a crisis of faith? When everything we believe is challenged? That's when we must discover (or re-discover) God's purpose for our life and learn to live with a mindset of His grace…grace that reveals His glory. This devotional will refresh believers in the gospel and encourage them to live every day so that the glory of God will be proclaimed by the power of grace at work in their lives.

Just Pray: 30 Days Of Encouragement (God's Not Done With You)
ISBN: 9780999131886 / List Price $9.99
Do you feel unqualified or ineffective in God's kingdom work? If you find yourself thinking, "What good am I to the kingdom anymore?" this devotional is for you. We believe you are strategically and sovereignly positioned to have kingdom impact in this generation through a simple commitment to prayer. What would happen if every believer who is limited by their age, physical abilities or circumstances decided to focus their time and attention on seeking God's heart and pleading for God's Spirit to bring a fresh revival to our world? What if we all did that? God is not looking for people of strength and confidence. He is seeking those who know they are helpless and weak so that His strength and glory can be made magnified. No matter what your challenges or limitations, God still has work for you to do for the kingdom. Accept the challenge and *just pray*.

Give Me A Faith Like That (Old Testament)
ISBN: 9781733047883 / List Price $9.99
God is so gracious to preserve His Word, not only the doctrines and theology that guide our faith, but the real-life stories that inspire our faith. The individual, historical records of ordinary men and women in the Bible narrate in living color God's plan of redemption, which culminated in Jesus. We have a role to play in God's story, too. Ours may not be written down in scripture, but it is significant and important as we pass on our faith in the gospel of Jesus Christ to those around us. Come with me as we step into the lives of faithful men and women who lived before us. Let us learn our lessons well, for one day, we will all stand around God's throne, from the first generation to the last, together worshipping the One in whom our faith rests.

About The Author

Sheila Alewine came to Christ at an early age, growing up in a Baptist church in Western North Carolina. She met her husband, Todd, while attending Liberty University in Lynchburg, VA; they married in 1985 and have spent their lives serving God together while raising two daughters.

Sheila fell in love with Bible study when asked to join a Precept study as a young mom. Throughout the years of raising their daughters, working full-time and serving in ministry, she has loved studying and teaching in the Word. Currently enjoying the "empty-nest" stage of life, she writes to encourage believers in their faith journey and kingdom work.

Sheila and her husband reside in Hendersonville, NC, where they have established *Around The Corner Ministries* to equip and encourage followers of Christ to share the gospel where they live, work and play. They love spending time with their daughters, sons-in-law, and grandchildren.

Connect with Sheila at her blog at *sheilaalewine.com*.

Contact Us

If this devotional has made an impact on your life, please let us know by contacting us through our website **aroundthecornerministries.org**, by email to sheila@aroundthecornerministries.org, or through our Facebook page.

Around The Corner Ministries exists to take the gospel to every neighborhood in America. Our mission is to equip followers of Jesus to engage their neighborhoods and communities with the gospel of Jesus Christ.

Around The Corner Ministries is a partner to the local church, designed to teach and train Christ-followers how to evangelize their neighborhoods, workplaces, and communities. The goal is to grow healthy local churches filled with mature believers who are comfortable and passionate about sharing their faith. If you would like more information on how our ministry can partner with your local church, please contact us.

Notes

[1] Blueletterbible.org
[2] https://www.scienceabc.com/humans/the-human-brain-vs-supercomputers-which-one-wins.html

www.ingramcontent.com/pod-product-compliance
Lightning Source LLC
Chambersburg PA
CBHW052116070526
44584CB00017B/2515